# Make Your Own
# SOUTHERN BELLE CLOTH DOLL
# and Her Wardrobe

Claire Bryant



DOVER PUBLICATIONS, INC.
Mineola, New York

This book is dedicated to all my relatives, past and present,
for whom the dolls were named.

*Copyright*



Published in Canada by General Publishing Company, Ltd., 30 Lesmill Road, Don Mills, Toronto, Ontario.
Published in the United Kingdom by Constable and Company, Ltd., 3 The Lanchesters, 162–164 Fulham Palace Road, London W6 9ER.

*Bibliographical Note*

*Make Your Own Southern Belle Cloth Doll and Her Wardrobe* is a new work, first published by Dover Publications, Inc., in 1999.

*Library of Congress Cataloging-in-Publication Data*

Bryant, Claire.
Make your own Southern Belle cloth doll and her wardrobe/ Claire Bryant.
p. cm.
ISBN 0-486-40483-8 (pbk.)
1. Dollmaking. 2. Cloth dolls. 3. Doll clothes Patterns. I. Title.
TT175.B795 1999
745.592'21—dc21 99-23441
CIP

Manufactured in the United States of America
Dover Publications, Inc., 31 East 2nd Street, Mineola, N.Y. 11501

# Introduction

Dollmaking can become an addiction. Once I began to make these dolls, I was unable to stop until I had completed an entire extended family of southern belles. I am sure your cast of characters will be different, but let me introduce you to mine.

**Bonnie Jean**, the bride, is very much in love with her fiancé, Ernest, a lieutenant in the Confederate Army. He didn't want to wear his uniform for the wedding, but Bonnie Jean insisted . . . and she usually gets her way!

**Myrna Ann**, the bridesmaid, is very glad her older sister is getting married, because she knows she will be next. Her beau, Vernon, plans to ask her father for her hand right after Bonnie Jean's wedding.

**Alice Genevieve**, Bonnie Jean's youngest sister is dressed for a garden party. Her friends call her Genny, and her daddy calls her his "little flower" because she loves to spend hours in the garden. She also loves to do needlework and crocheted her own flower basket.

**Louise Matilda**, dressed in plaid wants to be a secretary. She is very practical and doesn't wear crinolines because she thinks they are silly. Secretly, she wishes she was getting married like her cousin, Bonnie Jean. Every night when she says her prayers, she asks God to send her a man . . . as soon as possible.

Cousin **Mary Jane** is dressed for the engagement ball. She loves to get dressed up and takes hours to prepare for a ball. She wants to have everything match and goes to great trouble and expense to have her shoes match her dress. She is also a dreadful flirt!

**Shirley Louise**, Mary Jane's sister, is very fussy about what she wears. She has her own dressmaker and usually wears pleated trims and ruffles. She spends most of her time practicing the piano. If she isn't asked to play at a gathering, she is likely to pout for days.

Cousin **Jean Eleanor** loves to ride. When no one is looking, she throws her leg over the saddle and rides the way the boys do. Mama would have a fit if she knew!

Everyone loves **Hazel Magree**, the mother of the bride. She is dressed in black for the funeral of her elderly aunt. It will be cold at the cemetery, so she has a muff and cape to keep her warm.

# Making the Doll

## Materials:

1/2 yd. flesh-colored fabric. I used flannel because it has the "feel" of skin. Because I could not find the color I wanted, I used two colors of light-weight flannel, placing white over bright pink. I cut the two layers of fabric as one.
Thread to match fabric
Acrylic paint for facial features—gray, lavender, black, and pink
Small, fine paintbrush
Embroidery floss for facial features
Yarn, packaged mohair or synthetic hair, or doll wig
Polyester stuffing, 1 bag

## Pattern Pieces

A (head) — see instructions below
B (body) — cut 2
C (arm) — cut 4
D (leg) — cut 4
E (sole) — cut 2

## To Make

**Face**

It is easier to paint and embroider the face before cutting it out. Cut a 6" square of fabric and trace the head and features onto it. Using acrylic paints and a fine brush, paint the face following the photograph below and the diagram on Plate 1. Outline the eyes and top of lids with gray; fill in lids with lavender and the corners of the eyes with white. Fill the center with black, making the top not quite round where it "tucks under" the lid. Add a small pinkish-red dot in the corner of the eye closest to the nose. Nostrils can be either painted or stitched; if desired, make two dots for nose with pinkish red. Fill in the mouth with pinkish red.

After the paint is completely dry, embroider the face following the photograph below and the diagram on Plate 1. Outline the eye with one

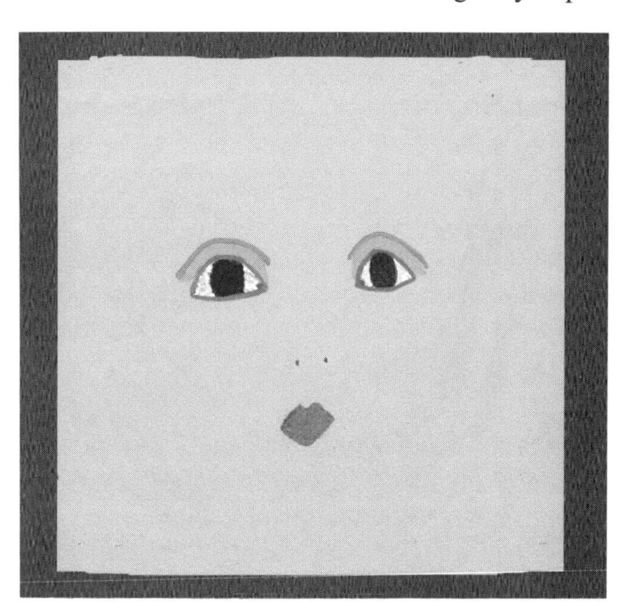

Painted Face

Embroidered Face

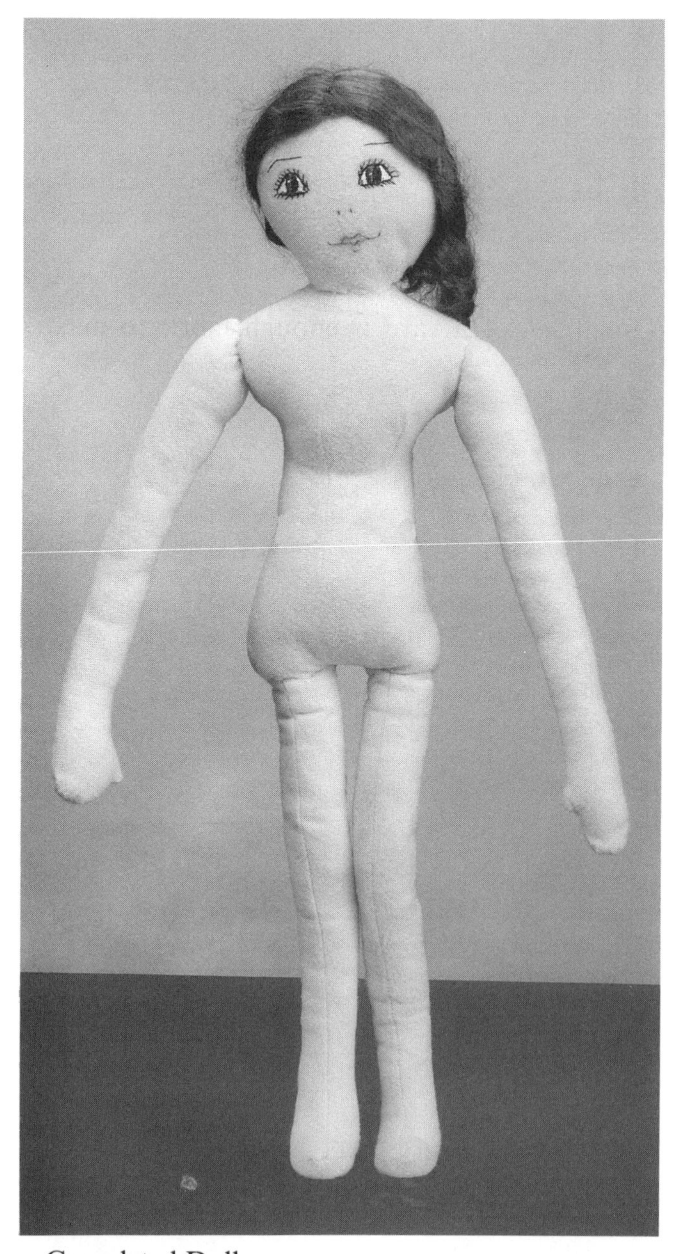

Completed Doll

strand of black or dark brown floss. Using two strands of desired eye color, cover the left half of the black center of each eye with satin stitch; add one small white stitch on top of this for a highlight. Add straight-stitch eyelashes, using 1 strand of black or dark brown. Stitch the eyebrows using 2 strands and 2 or 3 long straight stitches. You might want to practice on a spare piece of fabric to get the shape you want. Happy faces tend to have more arched brows.

Stitch the mouth with long dark flesh or light brown straight stitches. Add straight-stitch nostrils.

**Assembling the Doll**

Cut out face, back of head, bodies, arms, and legs. *Note*: All pattern pieces include ¼" seam allowance.

Right sides together, sew darts in face, body, and arms (if desired). Stitch face and back of head together, leaving base open. Clip curves and turn right side out. Stuff head firmly. Stitch front and back of body together leaving open at base. Clip curves and turn right side out. Stuff firmly. Stitch legs and arms together in pairs, leaving top open for stuffing. Stitch bottom of foot in place, matching single notch to toe and double notch to heel. Clip curves and turn pieces right side out. Stuff the hands lightly, and, if desired, backstitch three lines along hand to indicate fingers. Finish stuffing arms; stuff legs.

Place head over neck and blindstitch in place. Blindstitch arms to body. Blindstitch legs in place, closing the bottom of the body as you attach the legs.

Firm stuffing makes all the difference to the appearance of your doll, so you may want to add additional stuffing with a chopstick or knitting needle as you join the parts.

# Making the Clothes

Usually, ¾ of a yard is enough fabric to make any of the dresses, however, if the dress has a lot of ruffles you will need 1 yard. I usually buy 2 to 3 yards of trim or ruffling. Use cottons or blends for the "day" dresses and taffeta or satin for ball gowns and bridal gowns. Follow the photographs for the number of ruffles, trim ideas, and so forth.

I used ¼" seams throughout (included in pattern pieces). I found that it was easier to line the tops of the dresses, making enclosed edges at the neck, back, and lower edges, rather than turning and hemming such small areas. If you are making the clothes entirely by hand, you may not want to line the tops. I added the trim before sewing the seams and included the trim right in the seam. If you are using a fabric that ravels easily, be sure to finish the edges of the seams, either by overcasting, or with a machine zigzag stitch.

It is easier to dress the doll if the bodices and skirts are made separately. I made casings for the skirts, and used heavy crochet thread for cords. Buttons on the ends of the cords will keep them from getting lost in the casing. If you prefer not to use casings, you can attach the skirt directly to the bodice.

All of the dolls wear pantaloons. Most wear crinolines rather than the traditional hoop skirt, as they are easier to make and easier to pack when the doll is stored. Crinolines can be made of any fabric with either ruffled lace, net, or pre-ruffled trim added in rows to help the skirts stand out. I used an antique linen sheet that was torn beyond repair. It provided lots of fabric for dolly undergarments.

The "bust improver," or corset top, was added so that a dolly (Mary Jane was asking) could have cleavage to show off her garment. Most of the girls preferred to go *au naturel*.

I discovered that my local discount department store and crafts chain store had lots of choices for finishing the doll. Not only did they have wired pearls, fancy trim, ruffles, and feathers, but they also had bags of hair in many colors. Doll shoes are available in a variety of sizes. I made some shoes of fabric or felt and have included a pattern. The easiest ones are knitted or crocheted. See directions on page 5.

It is easier to try on the clothes and dress the doll before you add the wig. Some patterns may have to be adjusted since the amount of stuffing can vary the doll's shape considerably.

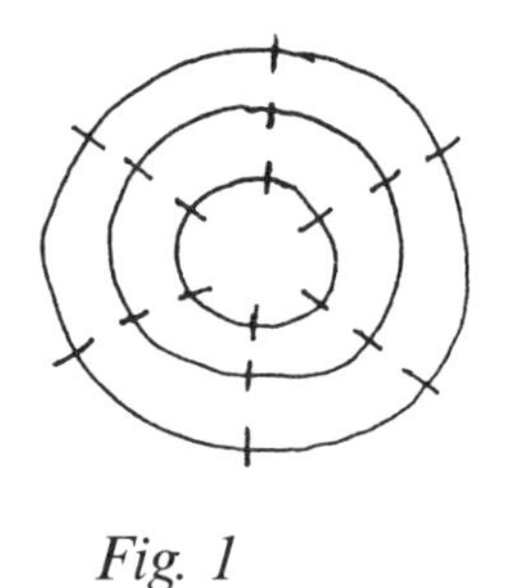

*Fig. 1*

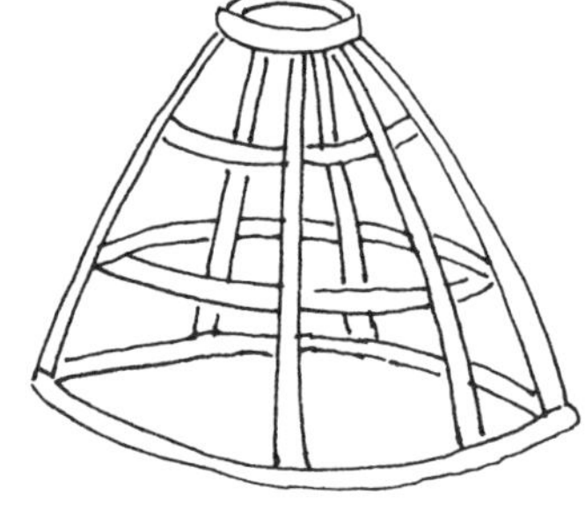

*Fig. 2*

**Hoop skirt**
Use the inner portion of wooden embroidery hoops. You will need 7", 9", and 12"-diameter hoops. Wrap each one with twill tape; fasten with glue or tack with thread. Place the hoops on a flat surface and mark across as shown in *Fig. 1*. Cut one piece of twill tape for the waistband. Cut six more pieces each 11½" long. Tack these to the waistband and to the hoops following *Fig. 2*. Sew a hook and eye to waistband, adjusting to fit.

**Crinoline**
Cut skirt 14" x 34". Fold under and stitch ¼" along bottom of skirt piece.

If you are using net for the ruffles, cut 4 ruffles 6" x 52". Fold in half lengthwise and press. Gather ¼" from raw edge. Apply the ruffles starting about 2" from the bottom hem. Overlap the ruffles about ½" as you progress upwards towards the waist. Topstitch to the skirt. Adjust the length from the top at this time. Fold the top edge over ¼" twice and stitch to make casing. Run heavy crochet thread or cord through the casing and tie a button on each end so it will not slip through.

**Pantaloons**
Cut 4 of pattern P1. Sew the side seams. Before sewing the inside seams, hem the bottom of the legs, adding ruffles and trim. Stitch the inside seam, stitching up one leg, around the crotch, and down the other leg. Fold the top over ¼" twice and stitch for casing. Run a drawstring through the casing, tying a button on each end.

**Bust improver**
Cut 2. Baste narrow lace or trim along top edge of one piece, matching raw edges. Stitch pieces together along all edges, leaving an opening for turning at the bottom. Clip curves and turn right side out. Stuff upper portion lightly with polyester stuffing; topstitch along broken lines to hold stuffing in place. Slipstitch opening. Sew hooks and eyes to back edges, adjusting to fit.

**Skirts**
Follow the picture to see the placement of ruffles. The individual instuctions will tell you how many ruffles and how wide to make them. Hem skirt by hand or machine or add ruffle as in directions. Stitch back seam. Try skirt on the doll and adjust the length from the top, allowing ½" for casing. Fold over top of skirt top ¼" twice; stitch to form a casing. Run a drawstring through the casing and tie a button on each end.

**Bodice**
Cut 2. Place right sides together and stitch around the neck, back, and lower edges. Trim, clip curves, and turn right side out. Press. Add snaps or hooks and eyes at center back.

**Bodice with cap sleeves**
The sleeves are part of the bodice pattern. Cut 4, cut 2 of the pieces along the center line for backs. Stitch backs to front at shoulders; repeat with lining. Stitch bodice to lining along neck, back, and lower edges, and along armhole edges to notch marked on pattern. Clip curves and at notches and turn right side out. Sew darts in front through both layers. Sew side seams up to notch. Trim sleeves with ruffles and lace trim. Let the trim hang over the sleeve edge. Sew snaps or hooks and eyes at center back.

**Sleeve**
Cut 2.

*Sleeve (1)*: Narrow hem sleeve at wrist edge. Cut elastic (stretched) the length of the doll's wrist plus ½". Hold one end of the elastic firmly and stretch it across the bottom of the sleeve 1/4" above hem. Stitch elastic in place, gathering sleeve as you stitch. The ends will be caught in the seam. Gather the sleeve top and pin it to the bodice, easing the gathers to fit. Stitch in place. Sew sleeve seam from wrist up to armhole and down side of bodice.

*Sleeve (2)*: Narrow hem sleeve at wrist edge; sew trim across edge. Insert sleeve as in (1).

### Cape

Cut cape and lining. Stitch around entire piece, leaving an opening large enough for turning. Clip curves, turn right side out and press. Close opening by hand. Add tie, button and loop, or hook and eye at neck. Trim with braid, or embroider with featherstitch.

### Shoes

Use patterns S1 and S2. For fabric, cut 4 tops and 2 soles. For felt, cut 2 tops and 2 soles. Seam the back edges together, matching A to B. For fabric shoes, stitch top pieces together along top edge. Turn right side out and attach to sole. I found this easier to do if I basted the seam first. The felt will not ravel, so does not have to be lined. See below for knitted or crocheted shoes.

### Hair

I used a wide variety of materials for the dolls' hair. Nylon or acrylic hair, both straight and curly, is widely available in crafts shops. Follow the manufacturer's directions for purchased hair. Use matching thread to stitch the hair to the head.

For yarn wigs, wrap the yarn around a book or piece of cardboard to get the desired length; cut at one side. Place the strands across the doll's head and stitch a center part. Pull the hair down and to the sides.

Braids, whether yarn or other fiber, were made separately and stitched on top of the hair that was already in place. The pearls in Bonnie Jean's braid came on a wire. They were cut into 1" lengths and tucked into the braid.

### Jewelry and other accessories

Old pins, buttons, and trim make lovely additions to the doll clothes. Tiny baskets, lockets, fans, and other accessories add to the charm of your dolls. Keep all accessories small so that they do not overpower the doll. Beads make great earrings for the dolls. If the dolls are for adults or older children, and you want to make the earrings removable, use pins to attach them to the head. **Do not use pins on dolls meant for young children.** Earrings can also be sewn to the head.

Charms and larger beads can be used for doll necklaces. Sew to ribbon or thread onto string and tie around the doll's neck.

### Knitting and Crochet Directions

*Shoes* are made of a rectangular piece, either crocheted or knitted. Chain or cast on the length of the foot, work back and forth until piece will fit down one side of the foot, across the bottom, and an equal distance up the other side. Cast off or finish crocheting, and seam each end and partially across the top of the shoe. These shoes will fit snuggly to the foot.

*Reticules (purses)* are made with crochet cotton and a size 4 or 5 steel crochet hook. Start with a chain of 4, join to form a ring, then work single crochet around and around, increasing in every other stitch by working two sc's in a space instead of one. When the bottom is the size you want, work up the side, around and around without increasing, in either single or double crochet. Make one row of dc to run a drawstring through. Chain the desired length for the drawstring.

# Bonnie Jean

## Bride

### Materials

White taffeta for gown
White fabric for crinoline and pantaloons
Net for pantaloon ruffles
½ yd. tulle for veil
3 yds. 1"-wide pre-gathered ribbon trim
2 yds. 1¼"-wide lace trim
1½ yds. lace trim with pearls
2 yds. satin rosebud trim
Scrap of cardboard for book
Wired pearls for necklace and hair trim
8 small pearls for earrings
Snaps
String for drawstrings
Buttons for drawstrings
Yarn for hair

### Pattern Pieces

BJ1 (bodice) — cut 4. Cut 2 pieces along center line for backs.
Cut underskirt 14" x 34"
See below for underskirt.

### To Make

Make pantaloons and crinoline following general instructions.

**Bodice**
Sew bodice with cap sleeves to lining following general instructions. For sleeves, cut 8"-long pieces of gathered ribbon and sew to arm edge of bodice. Sew side seams. Sew two rows of gathered ribbon around neck by hand; adding lace trim under top row. Sew rosebud trim over ribbon. Add snaps.

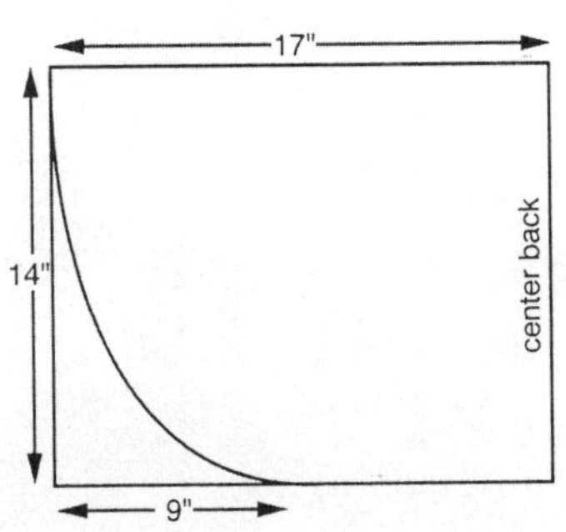


*Fig. 1*

**Underskirt**
Hem underskirt and sew back seam following general instructions. Sew two rows of gathered ribbon around lower edge, adding lace under top row. Sew rosebud trim over top edges of ribbon. Complete skirt as in general instructions.

**Overskirt**
Cut overskirt 14" x 34"; shape front edges following *Fig. 1.* Press under ¼" on front and lower edges of overskirt; sew lace and pearl trim over edge. Make casing following general instructions.

**Veil**
Cut an 18" x 36" oval of tulle for veil. Cut 12" of ribbon trim. Sew ends together to form a circle; run a gathering thread around inner edge. Place veil over head. Place circle of ribbon on top; pull up gathers to fit. Secure ends and pin veil to ribbon. Remove from doll and tack ribbon in place. Secure veil to head with bobby pins.

**Finishing**
Make yarn hair, adding a coronet of braids. Place wired pearls in hair.

For prayer book, cut a 2" by 3" rectangle of lightweight cardboard; cover with white paper. Cut two 6" lengths of rosebud trim. Fold book in half, placing trim inside with ends hanging out.

Make pearl earrings by stringing a pearl on thread, then inserting both ends of thread through eye of needle; add 3 more pearls. Cut a 4" length of wired pearls for necklace.

# Myrna Ann
## Bridesmaid

### Materials

Pink gingham check for skirt and scarf lining
White eyelet for bodice, scarf, pantaloons, and crinoline
Solid white for bodice lining and bust improver
Gathered eyelet trim for crinoline
Narrow lace or trim for bust improver
½" yd. ½"-wide eyelet beading for sleeve trim
5 yds. embroidered trim for skirt ruffles
½ yd. 1"-wide lace edging
½ yd. ⅛"-wide pink satin ribbon for sleeve trim
½ yd. 1"-wide white satin ribbon
¾ yd. ¼"-wide grosgrain ribbon
1 ft. 1/16" wide pink satin ribbon
Artificial flowers for hair
Small bouquet of artificial flowers
Scrap of cardboard
Floral tape
Fabric glue
3 pink beads
8 pearls for earrings
Snaps
String for drawstrings
Buttons for drawstrings
Synthetic curls for doll's hair

### Pattern Pieces

MA1 (bodice) — cut 2
MA2 (sleeve) — cut 2
MA3 (scarf) — cut 1 each from eyelet and gingham
Cut skirt 12" x 34"
Cut six skirt ruffles 5" by 40"

### To Make

Following general instructions, make pantaloons and crinoline of eyelet, using gathered eyelet trim for crinoline ruffles. Make bust improver.

**Bodice**
Make bodice following general instructions. For each sleeve, cut a 1¾"-wide strip of gingham; turn under ¼" on each long edge; press. Pin strip across sleeve with lower edge about 3½" above lower edge of sleeve. Stitch along pressed edges. Stitch eyelet beading over gingham strip. Finish bodice, following instructions for Sleeve (1). Starting at center of sleeve, thread ⅛"-wide satin ribbon through beading; tie ends in a bow.

**Skirt**
Fold skirt ruffles in half lengthwise and press. Stitch embroidered trim along folded edge of each ruffle. Follow basic skirt directions, adding ruffles as for crinoline.

**Scarf**
Stitch scarf to lining, leaving an opening for turning. Turn, press, and slipstitch opening. Cut two 12" lengths of grosgrain ribbon. Turn under one end of each length and sew to points of scarf. Place scarf around doll's neck, cross ends over in front and wrap them to the back, tying ribbon in a bow. Let the ends of the ribbon hang down. Fold over the front edges of the scarf so that the lining shows.

**Bouquet**
Cut a 3" circle of cardboard; cut a hole in center (one end of a bolt of ribbon works well for this). With lace edging on bottom, baste white ribbon and edging together. Pleat or gather ribbon and lace and glue to edge of cardboard. Place bouquet of flowers through hole in cardboard; wrap stems with floral tape beneath cardboard base. Wrap stems around doll's hand. You can safety pin the doll's hands together so that she can hold the bouquet in both hands.

**Finishing**
Place sprigs of flowers in hair, attaching with bobby pins.

For earrings, string a pearl onto thread; then place both ends of thread through eye of needle. Sew to doll's head. For necklace, thread beads onto 1/16"-wide ribbon; tie around doll's neck.

# Alice Genevieve
## Garden Party

### Materials

Dotted swiss for dress
Fabric for pantaloons and crinoline
Net for crinoline ruffles
4 yds. embroidered trim
¾" yd. ¾"-wide grosgrain ribbon for sash
Cardboard for hat
Fabric glue
White crochet thread for basket
Size 4 or 5 steel crochet hook
Starch for basket
Plastic wrap to shape basket
Artificial flowers
8 pearls for earrings
2 small buttons for earrings
Wired pearls for necklace
Snaps
String for drawstrings
Buttons for drawstrings
Long synthetic curls for hair

### Pattern Pieces

AG1 (dress top) — cut 2
AG2 (sleeve) — cut 2
AG3 (hat) — cut 2 from fabric, 1 from cardboard
Cut skirt 12" x 34"
Cut skirt ruffle 6" x 56"
Cut 2 bodice ruffles 4" x 20"

### To Make

Make undergarments following general instructions.

**Bodice**
Sew bodice to lining following general instructions. Hand sew embroidered trim around neck edge. Press under ¼" on wrist edge of each sleeve; sew 2 rows of trim across sleeve, one at folded edge and one about 3" above fold. Complete sleeves following Sleeve (1) instructions. Sew in sleeves and sew side seams. Sew bodice ruffles together along all edges, leaving an opening for turning. Turn right side out and slipstitch opening. Stitch trim along one edge; gather other edge ¼" in from edge. Topstitch ruffle around neck edge. Sew on snaps.

**Skirt**
Press under 1" on one long edge of skirt ruffle. Run a gathering thread ¾" from folded edge. Turn under ¼" twice on other edge of ruffle and stitch. Lap ruffle over lower edge of skirt by 1", baste in place over gathering. Add embroidered trim over basting; topstitch through all layers. Sew back seam and complete following general instructions.

**Hat**
Glue fabric to both sides of cardboard hat; glue trim around inner and outer edges.

**Basket**
Chain 4, join to form a ring. Work single crochet around and around, increasing in every other stitch by working two sc's in a space instead of one, until piece is 1¾" in diameter. Ch 3, work 2 dc in next st. Continue around in dc, increasing in every 3rd stitch until piece is 3" in diameter. *Ch 4, skip 2 dc, dc in next dc; repeat around. On next row, *Ch 4, dc in next ch-4 sp; repeat around. Work 2 rows of sc, working sc in each st and 5 sc in each ch-4 sp. For handle, attach thread in any st, sc in same st and in next 2 sc. Ch 1 turn. Continue to work back and forth in sc until handle measures 8½". Fasten off and sew to opposite side of basket. Starch basket heavily. Roll plastic wrap; place inside basket to hold shape. Allow basket to dry.

**Finishing**
Sew long synthetic curls over head, allowing them to hang free in the back.

Sew 4 pearls to small button; sew to head for earring; repeat on other side. Cut 4" length of wired pearls; place around doll's neck.

Dress doll, tucking bodice inside skirt. Tie sash around waist. Place hat on head, pulling loose curls through hole in crown of hat. Place flowers in basket; place basket over arm.

# Louise Matilda

## Plaid Ensemble

### Materials

Plaid fabric for skirt, scarf, and capelet
White fabric for blouse and petticoat
Red fabric for pantaloons and cape lining
2½ yds. bias tape for trim
Hook and eye
Snaps
String for drawstrings
Buttons for drawstrings
Red crochet thread for reticule
Purchased doll eyeglasses
Yarn for hair

### Pattern Pieces

LM1 (blouse) — cut 4. Cut 2 pieces along center line for backs.
LM2 (sleeve) — cut 2
LM3 (cuff) — cut 2
LM 4 (capelet) — cut 1 each from plaid and lining
Cut skirt 14" by 34"
Cut petticoat 13" x 34"

### To Make

Make red pantaloons following general instructions. Make petticoat following general instructions for skirt.

**Blouse**
Sew front to backs at shoulders; repeat with lining. Stitch lining to blouse at neck, back, and lower edges. Turn right side out. Do not sew darts in blouse front. Run a row of gathering stitches along lower edge of each sleeve. Wrong sides together, stitch cuff to sleeve, drawing up gathers to fit. Press seam towards cuff. Turn up ¼" on lower edge of cuff. Fold cuff in half to right side; topstitch over seam. Sew sleeves to blouse. Sew side seams. Sew snaps to center back.

**Skirt**
Hem one long edge of skirt. Sew bias tape across skirt, 1" above lower edge. Complete following basic instructions.

**Scarf**
Cut a square 12" x 12"; cut diagonally to form 2 triangles. Stitch bias binding aross two short edges of one triangle, mitering at point. Rights sides in, sew triangles together along short edges. Turn right side out. Bind long edge with bias binding.

**Capelet**
Make capelet following general instructions, sew on hook and eye.

**Finishing**
Sew on yarn hair following general instructions. Make a long braid of yarn, coil and tack to head. Crochet reticule following general instructions.

# Mary Jane
## Ball Gown

### Materials

Blue satin for bodice, skirt, stole, and hat
Black fabric for pantaloons and bust improver
Fabric, twill tape, and embroidery hoops for hoop skirt
1½ yds. wide black lace galloon for skirt trimming
¾ yds. ¼"-wide black lace edging
1 yd. wide black fringe
Small black feathers
Scrap of cardboard for fan
Snaps
String for drawstrings
Buttons for drawstrings
3 medium blue beads
¼ yd. ¼"-wide black ribbon
Synthetic braid for hair

### Pattern Pieces

MJ1 (bodice) — cut 4. Cut 2 pieces along center line for backs.
MJ2 (hat) — cut 2
MJ3 (fan) — cut 1 from cardboard
See below for skirt
Cut stole 6½" by 32"

### To Make

Make pantaloons, bust improver, and hoop skirt following general instructions.

**Bodice**
Sew bodice to lining following general instructions. Hand sew lace around neck and armhole edges on wrong side. Sew side seams. Turn up ¼" on lower edge, stitch. Sew on snaps.

**Skirt**
For skirt, cut bottom ruffle 5" by 67", piecing fabric if necessary. Fold piece in half lengthwise; press and gather raw edges. Cut second ruffle 9" by 45". Right sides together, pin lower ruffle to one long edge of this piece, pulling up gathers to fit; stitch. Topstitch if desired. Hand sew lace galloon along lower edge of second ruffle. Cut top ruffle 4" by 36"; stitch second ruffle to one long edge. Try on skirt and adjust length to determine final width of top piece. Finish as in general instructions.

**Stole** (not shown)
Fold stole in half lengthwise and stitch raw edges, leaving an opening for turning. Turn right side out and slipstitch opening. Sew fringe to one long edge by hand.

**Hat**
Sew hat pieces together, leaving an opening for turning. Turn right side out; slipstitch opening. By hand, make a few gathering stitches along line indicated on pattern, draw up gathers, attaching feathers in stitching. Attach hat with bobby pins.

**Finishing**
Cover cardboard fan with colored paper or fabric, glue on feathers. Glue on thread loop to hang over Mary Jane's wrist.

Make black crocheted reticule. Sew blue bead to center of black ribbon; tie around doll's neck. Beginning at center back, coil braid around doll's head, holding in place with pins. Tuck end under previous coil. Tack in place and remove pins. A second layer of braid can be added if desired.

# Shirley Louise
## Visiting Costume

### Materials

Green taffeta for skirt, jacket, and bonnet
Off-white for dickey, pantaloons, and crinoline
Embroidered eyelet ruffling for crinoline and pantaloons
6" narrow lace for dickey
1 yd. 2"-wide lace for jacket and bonnet trim
2½ yds. purchased trim or 5½ yds. ⅝"-wide satin ribbon to match jacket (see below to make pleated trim)
Scrap of cardboard for parasol
Bias tape to match outfit
8" length ⅛"-diameter dowel
Button for parasol handle
String for drawstrings
Buttons for drawstrings
Snaps
Hook and eye
Smooth synthetic fiber for hair

### Pattern Pieces

SL1 (dickey) — cut 1
SL2 (jacket) — cut 2
SL3 (sleeve) — cut 2
SL4 (bonnet) — cut 2
SL5 (bow) — cut 2
SL6 (parasol) — cut 1 of heavy paper
Cut skirt 14" by 34"

### To Make

Make pantaloons and crinoline following general instructions, using eyelet ruffling for crinoline ruffles.

**Dickey**
Turn under and stitch raw edges of dickey; stitch narrow lace around neck edge. Sew snap to back edges.

**Jacket**
Line jacket as in general instructions. By hand, sew wide lace to inside of sleeve. Sew 2 rows of trim* around lower edge of sleeve. Sew in sleeves as in general instructions. Sew side seams. Sew trim* around outer edge of jacket; overlap ends, turning under end on top. Sew hook and eye to front edge of jacket so that edges just meet.

**Skirt**
Cut a 4" by 68" strip of taffeta, piecing as needed. Fold in half lengthwise and press. Pleat strip, making ¼" to ⅜" pleats ½" apart. Finished strip should be at least 34" long. Press under one long edge of skirt. Overlap folded edge of skirt over pleated ruffle and stitch in place. Complete skirt following general instructions. Sew trim* around lower edge of skirt about ½" above ruffle.

**Bonnet**
Stitch bonnet pieces together leaving an opening at back for turning. Turn right side out and slipstitch opening. Stitch trim* around *inside* edge of bonnet. Fold back edge of hat to right side so that trim shows. For ties, cut two 1¼" x 12" strips of taffeta; press under edges. Fold in half lengthwise and press; stitch along long edge. Stitch ties to corners of bonnet on inside. Place hat on doll's head, pleating back edge to fit; pin to hold. Remove bonnet; tack pleats. Cut an 8"-long piece of wide lace; place inside bonnet with scalloped edge extending past edge of bonnet about ½". Tack in place. Sew bow pieces together, leaving an opening for turning. Turn right side out and close opening. Form into bow and sew to back of hat.

**Finishing**
Wrap dowel with bias tape; glue in place. Wrap parasol around dowel and glue. Glue button to end of dowel.

Sew on hair; add bun at back.

*To make pleated trim, cut ⅝"-wide ribbon twice the desired length plus several inches. Pin one end of ribbon in place on garment. Sew one edge of ribbon in place by hand, making small (⅛" to 3/16") pleats ¼" apart along length of ribbon. Repeat on opposite edge of ribbon.

# Jean Eleanor

## Riding Habit

### Materials

Fabric for pantaloons
Striped fabric for bodice, skirt, and cuffs
Solid tan for sleeves and bodice lining
Tan corduroy for cape and hat
Solid aqua for cape lining
Brown embroidery floss for cape trim
1¾ yd. ¼" aqua grosgrain ribbon for trim
Snaps
String for drawstrings
Buttons for drawstrings
Purchased boots
Smooth synthetic fiber for hair

### Pattern Pieces

JE1 (bodice) — cut 2
JE2 (sleeve) — cut 2
JE3 (hat) — cut 2
JE4 (cape) — cut 1 each from corduroy and lining
See below for skirt

### To Make

**Bodice**
Cut a ¾" x 7" strip of the bodice fabric; fold in half lengthwise and press. Right sides together, baste this strip around neck edge of bodice. Sew bodice to bodice lining following general instructions. Sew ribbon over neck seam by hand, turning raw edges to inside of bodice. For each sleeve cuff, cut a 4"-wide strip of bodice fabric the width of the lower edge of the sleeve. Fold in half with 4"-long edges together. Matching raw edges, pin to right side of sleeve; stitch. Press seam towards sleeve; topstitch in place. With *wrong* side of each sleeve up, sew ribbon across each cuff (cuffs will be turned up). Sew sleeves to bodice. Stitch side and sleeve seams, reversing seam on cuffs. Sew snaps to back. Turn up cuffs.

**Skirt**
Skirt is two layered. Cut top layer 8" by 36", bottom layer 13" by 36". Hem one long edge of each piece, sewing ribbon over stitching on top layer. Sew back seams. Place the top skirt over the lower skirt and treat them as one layer. Complete following general instructions.

**Hat**
Stitch hat and lining together, leaving an opening for turning. Turn right side out and slipstitch opening. Cut two 2" by 8½" strips of striped fabric; stitch together leaving an opening for turning. Turn right side out; slipstitch opening. Gather one long edge. Place piece on head and draw up gathers to fit. Place hat on top of this, pleating back of hat to fit; pin pleats to hold. Remove and sew gathered strip inside hat. Tack pleats and add loops of grosgrain ribbon. Attach to head with bobby pins.

**Cape**
Using 6 strands of brown embroidery floss, couch design on cape. Stitch cape and lining together, leaving opening for turn. Turn right side out. Sew on hook and eye.

**Finishing**
To make riding crop, wrap a dowel stick with tape, making a loop for doll's wrist at one end and strips of the tape at the other. Glue in place.
Sew on hair, add separate braid.

# Hazel Magree

## Sunday Best

### Materials

Lightweight black wool for skirt, vest, cape, and hat
Black fabric for blouse, lining, and crinoline
Scrap of black net for veil
¾ yd. black net for crinoline
White cotton for pantaloons
1½ yds. black fur trim
1 yd. narrow black lace
Black embroidery floss
Small button
Small hook and eye
Snaps
String for drawstrings
Buttons for drawstrings
¼ yd. ¼"-wide elastic
16 black seed beads
2 small silver beads
Synthetic curls for hair

### Pattern Pieces

HM1 (bodice) — cut 2
HM2 (sleeve) — cut 2
HM3 (vest) — cut 2
HM4 (cape) — cut 1 of main fabric, 1 of lining
HM5 (hat) — cut 2
Cut skirt 14" x 34"

### To Make

Make pantaloons and crinoline following general instructions.

**Bodice**
Cut an 18" length of black lace and run a gathering thread along heading. Pin lace around neck edge of bodice, adjusting gathers to fit and extending lace down left center back edge about 1". Sew blouse and lining together following general instructions. Make sleeves following instructions for sleeve (1), adding a length of lace across lower edge of sleeve before adding elastic. Sew snaps to center back.

**Skirt**
Stitch fur to skirt by hand before sewing back seam. Complete following general instructions.

**Vest**
Sew shoulder seams of vest; repeat with lining. Sew vest to lining around neck, armhole, and lower edge; leave side edges open. Turn right side out. Sew side seams of vest only, leaving lining free. Turn under side edges of lining and slipstitch Sew hook and eye to center front edges at waist.

**Cape**
Using 3 strands of floss, work featherstitch embroidery along edges of cape. Add embroidery thread loop at right neck edge and sew small button to left neck edge. Sew cape and lining together following general instructions.

**Hat**
Sew hat pieces together leaving an opening for turning; turn and slipstitch opening. Sew fur on by hand. Cut a 14" diameter circle of net; tack center of net to center top of inside of hat. Cut two 12" lengths of black ribbon; tack one to each front corner of hat on wrong side, catching net in stitching.

**Muff**
Cut a 4" x 6" piece each of fur and lining fabric, stitch together leaving ends open. Turn right side out. Stitch ends of fur together, leaving lining free. Turn in one raw edge of lining and slipstitch over other end.

**Finishing**
For earrings, thread 4 seed beads, a silver bead, and 4 more seed beads onto thread; form loop and stitch to side of head. Repeat on other side.

# Nightgown and Robe

*Note:* Nightgown and robe use the same pattern pieces and are made very similarly. The nightgown opens in the back and the robe opens in the front.

## Materials

Solid color cotton for nightgown and nightcap
¾ yd. narrow lace for trim
Flannel or velour for robe
¾"-wide lace for trim
Snaps
¾ yd. bias tape
½ yd. ⅛" wide elastic

## Pattern Pieces

NR1 (back and front) — cut 2 for each garment; cut 1 each along center line (nightgown backs and robe fronts)
NR2 (sleeve) — cut 2 for each garment
NR3 (yoke) — cut 4 for each garment; cut 2 on broken line for backs
NR4 (nightcap) — cut 1

## To Make

**Gown**
Stitch the backs together, leaving 2" open at the top. Gather the top edge of the front and backs, turning under ¼" at center back edges. Stitch the front and backs to the lower edges of the yokes, pulling up gathers to fit. Stitch the front yoke to the back yokes at the shoulders. Repeat with yoke lining. Stitch the yoke to the yoke lining around neck and back edges. Turn right side out. Turn under ¼" on lower edge of yoke lining and slipstitch over seam. Matching raw edges, baste lace to armhole edges of yoke. Finish wrist edge of sleeve following sleeve (1) instructions, adding lace trim. Sew in sleeves and sew underarm seams. Hem lower edge. Sew on snaps.

**Robe**
Narrow hem center front edges. Complete as for nightgown.

**Nightcap** (not shown)
Press under ¼" on edge; sew lace over edge. Run a gathering thread around ½" from edge. Cut a 22" length of bias tape, pin around cap with outer edge ½" from edge. Turn under ends of tape and butt ends. Stitch along edge of tape to form a casing. Measure circumference of doll's head. Cut elastic this length minus ½". Thread elastic through casing; overlap ends and tack securely.

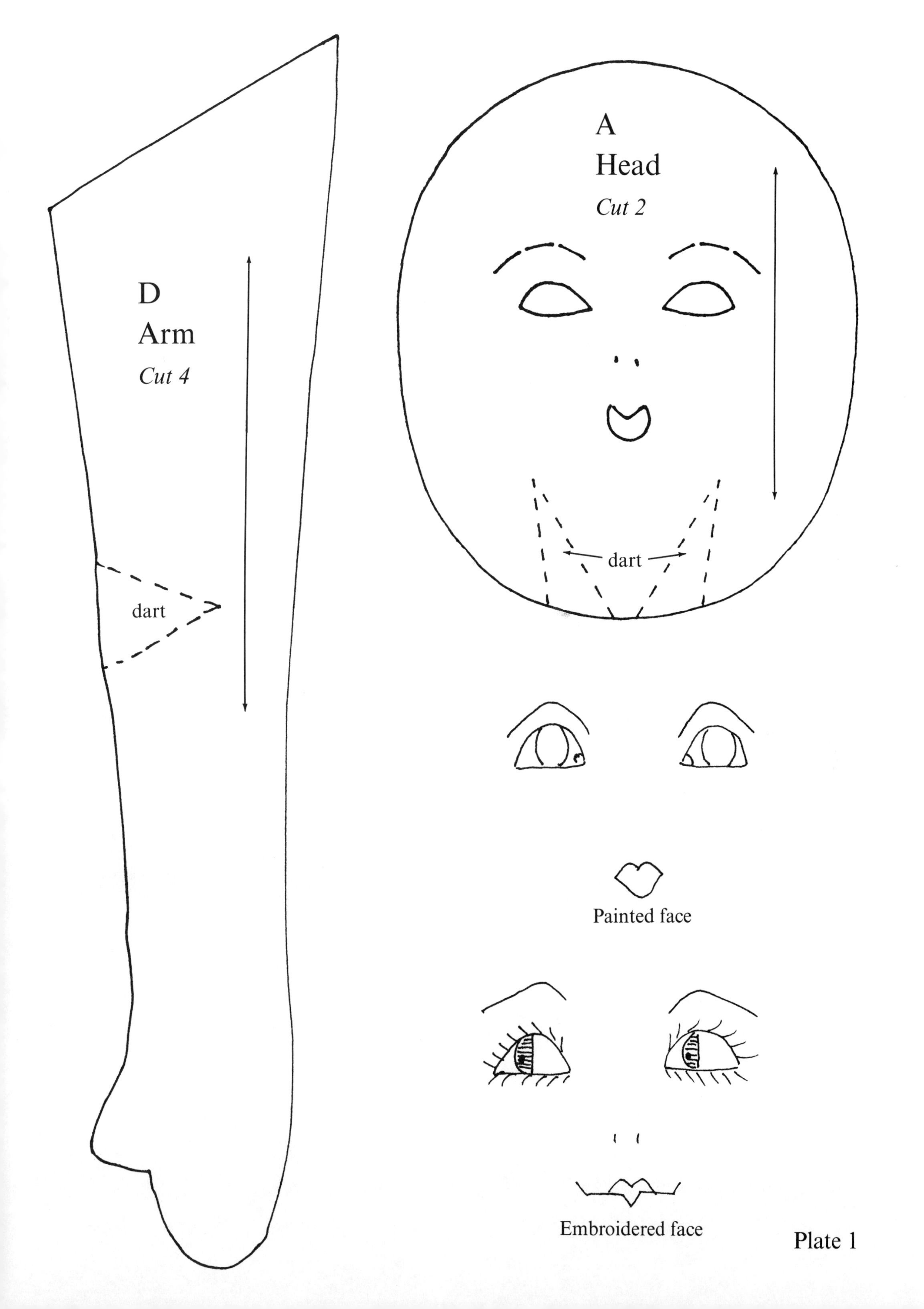
D
Arm
Cut 4
dart
A
Head
Cut 2
dart
Painted face
Embroidered face
Plate 1

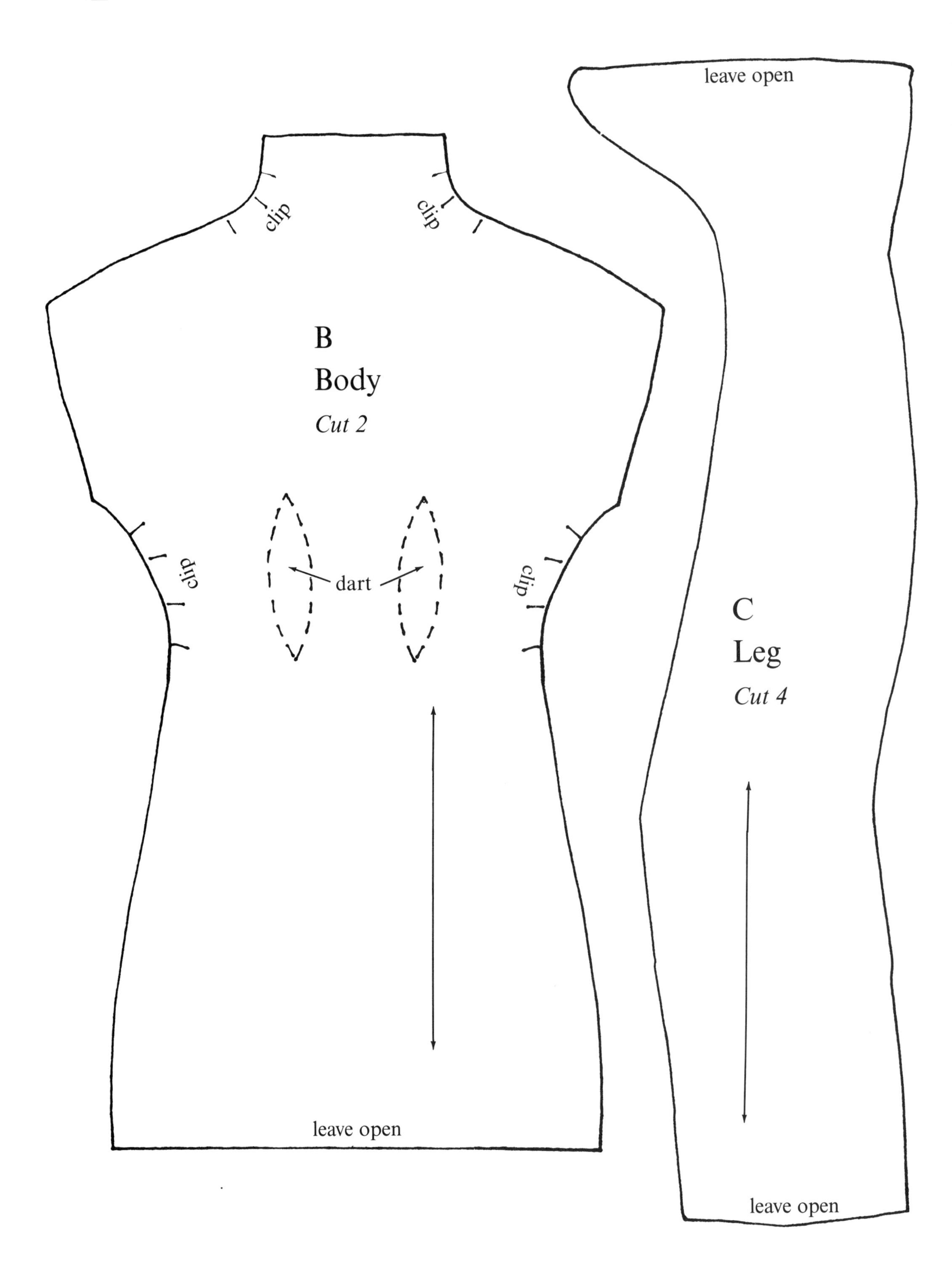
clip
clip
B
Body
Cut 2
dart
clip
clip
leave open
leave open
C
Leg
Cut 4
leave open

Plate 2

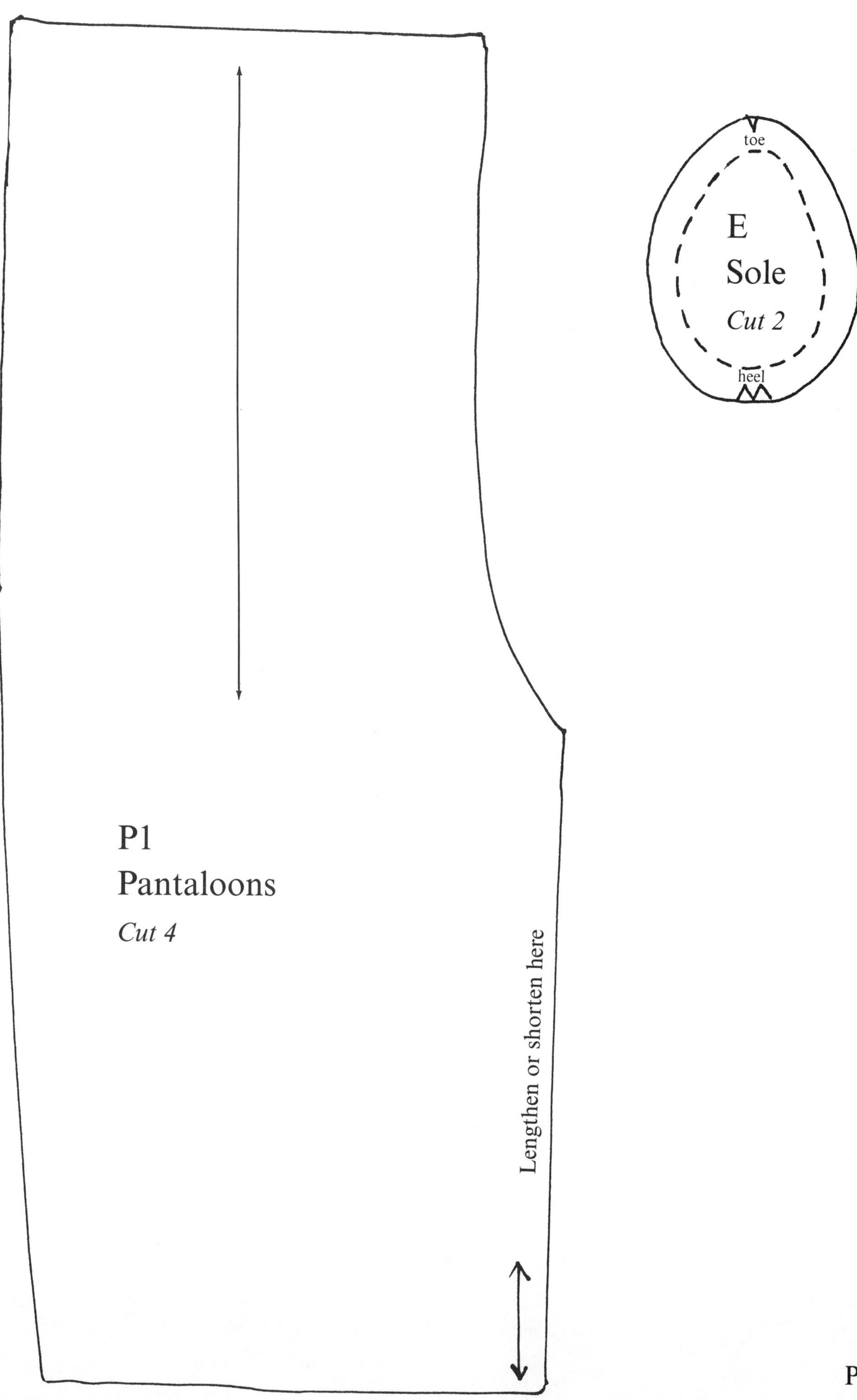
toe
E
Sole
Cut 2
heel
P1
Pantaloons
Cut 4
Lengthen or shorten here

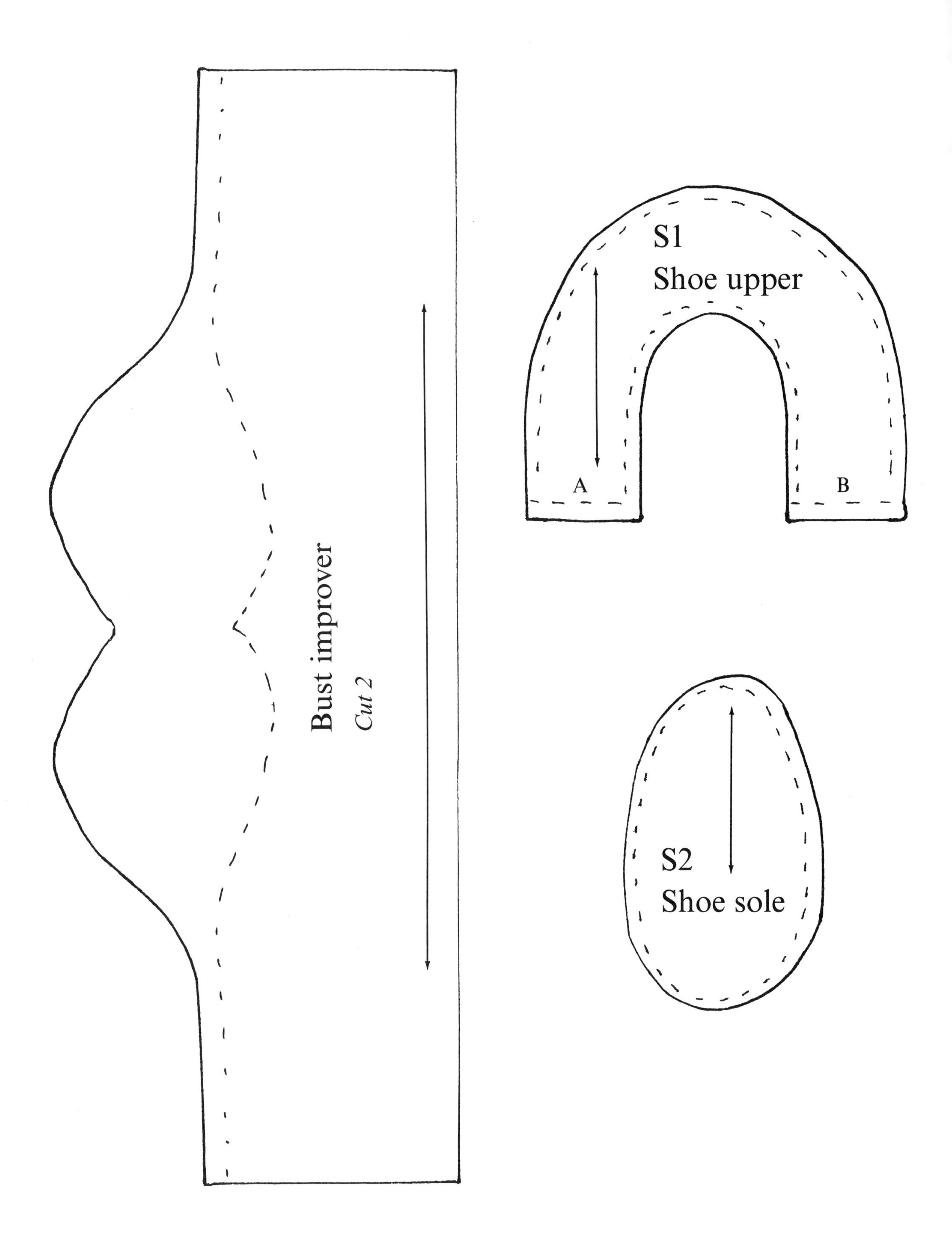


Plate 4

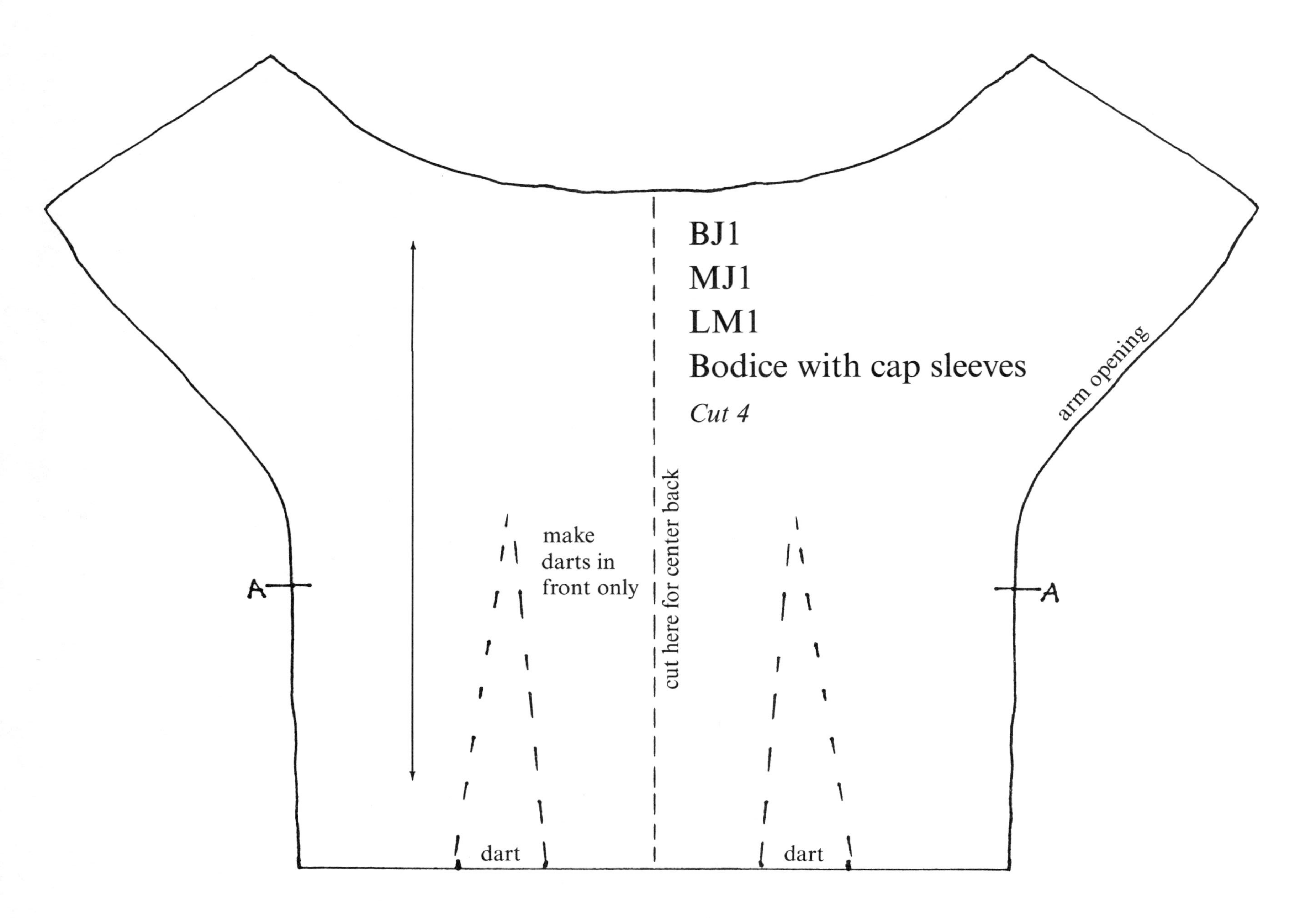
BJ1
MJ1
LM1
Bodice with cap sleeves
Cut 4
arm opening
make darts in front only
cut here for center back
A
A
dart
dart

Join the top of the pattern to the bottom
of the pattern, overlapping the shaded portion.

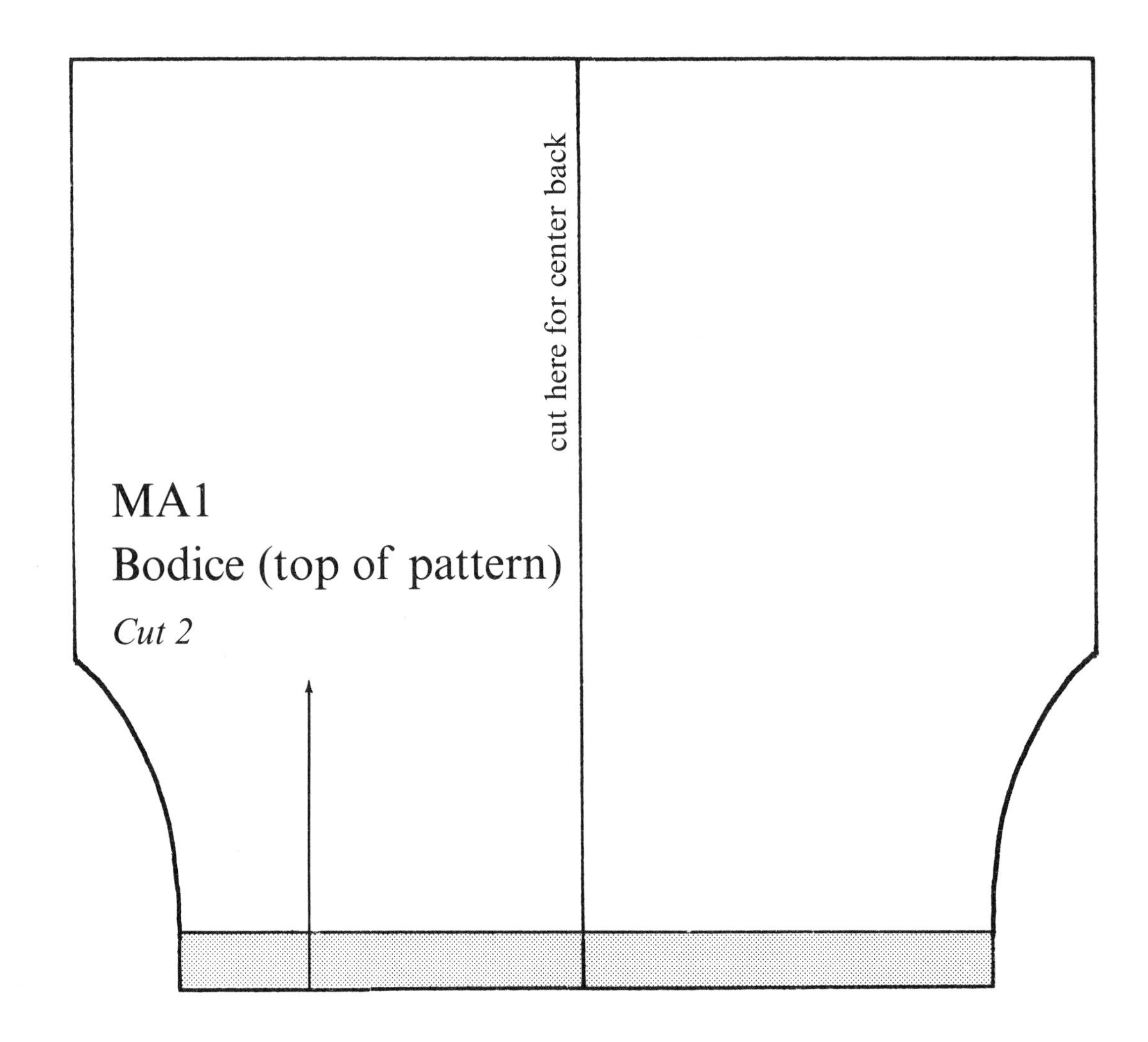

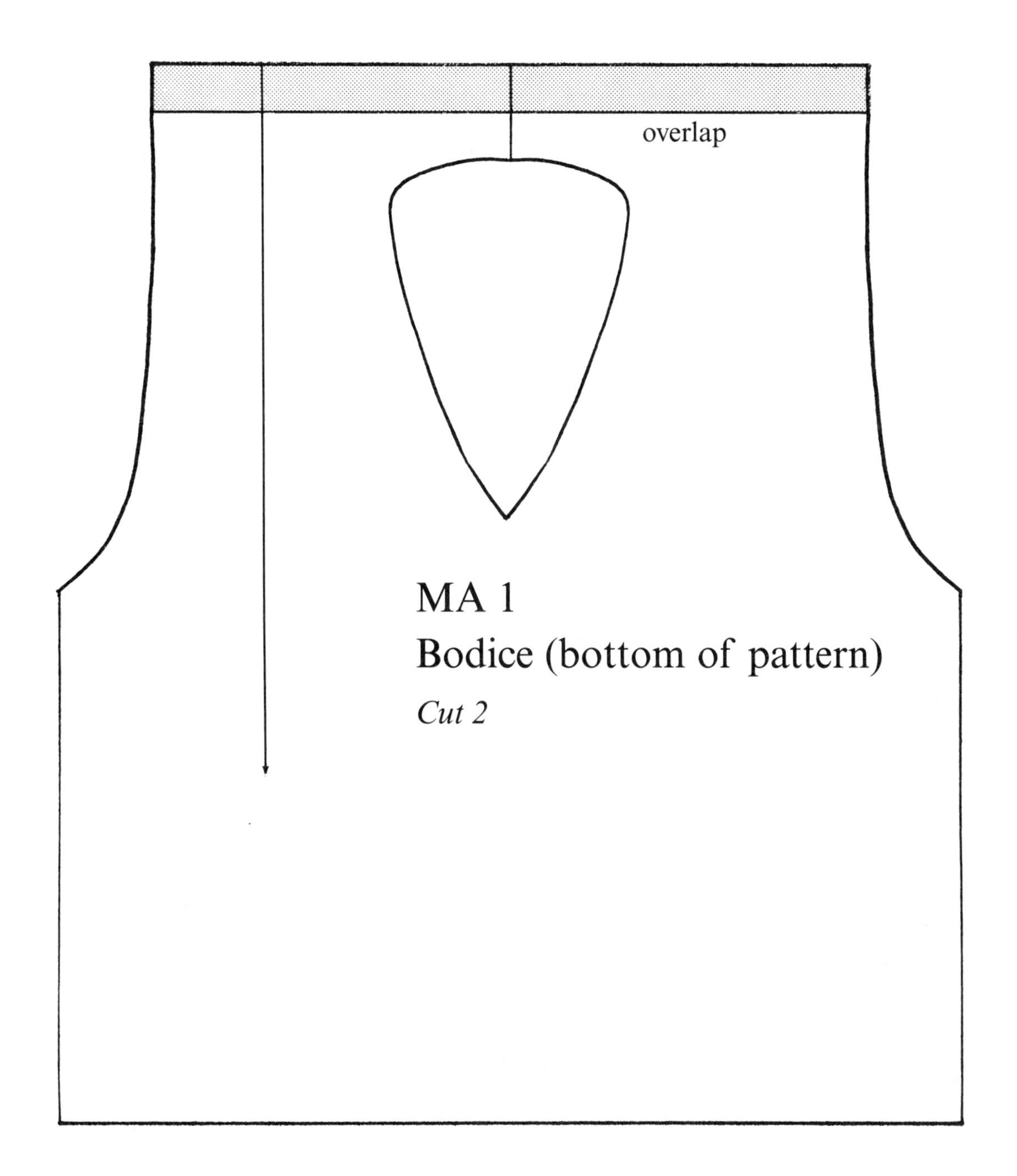
overlap
MA 1
Bodice (bottom of pattern)
Cut 2

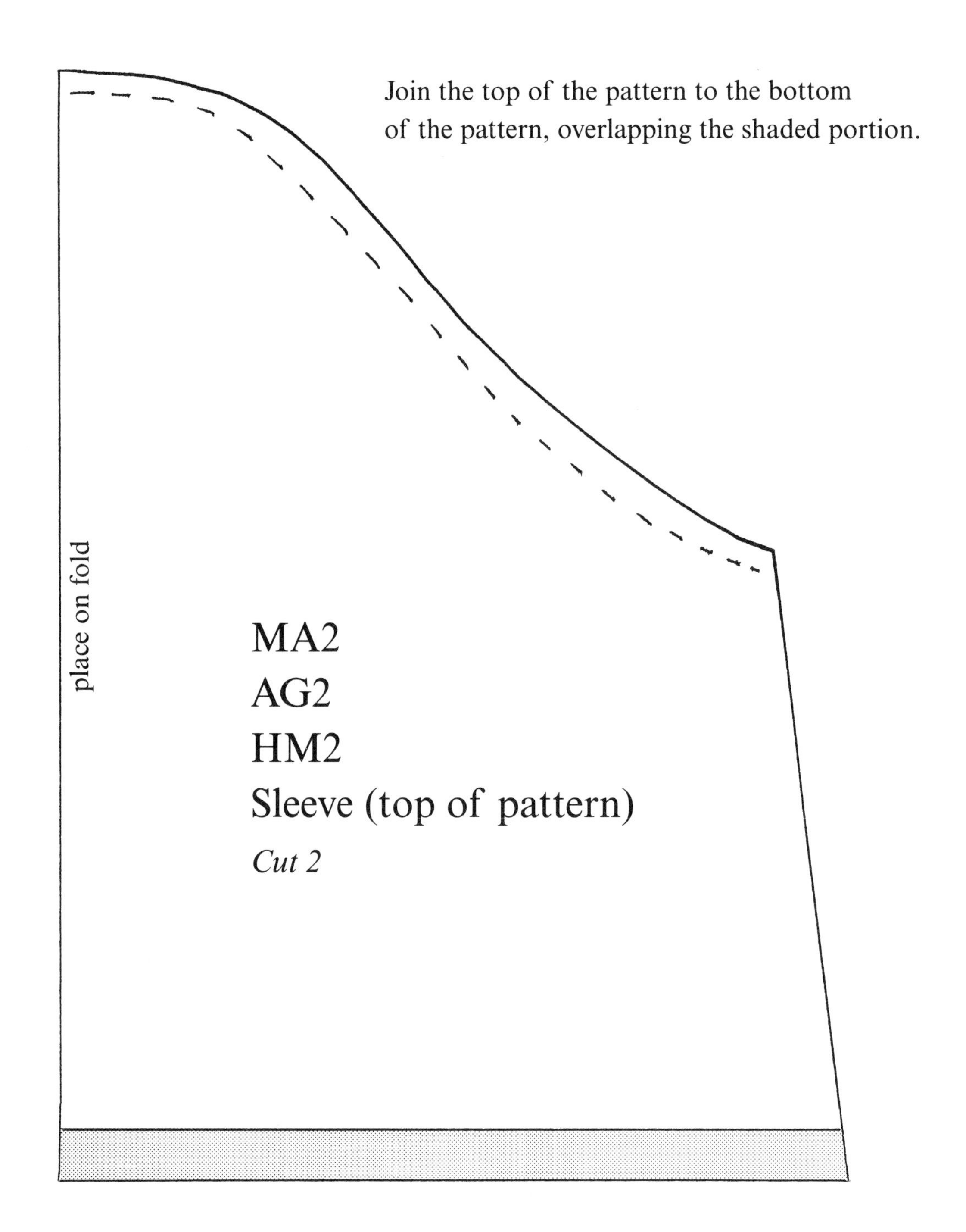
Join the top of the pattern to the bottom
of the pattern, overlapping the shaded portion.
place on fold
MA2
AG2
HM2
Sleeve (top of pattern)
Cut 2

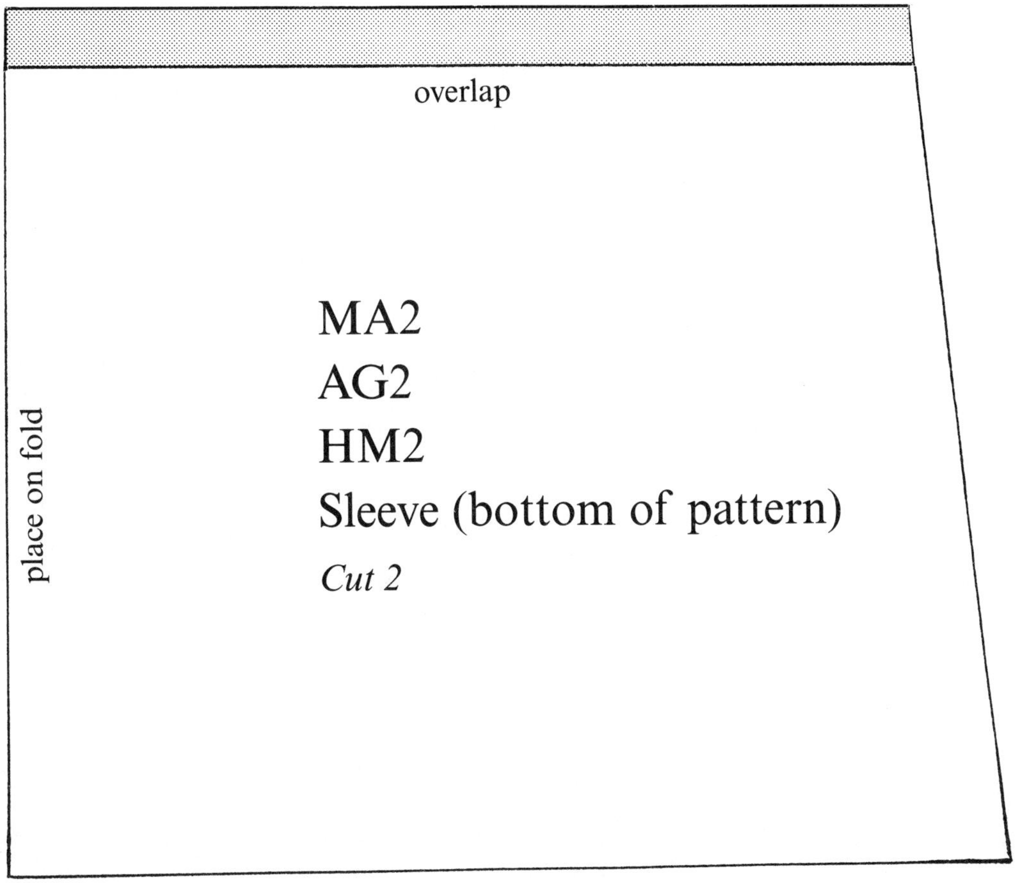

overlap

place on fold

MA2

AG2

HM2

Sleeve (bottom of pattern)

*Cut 2*

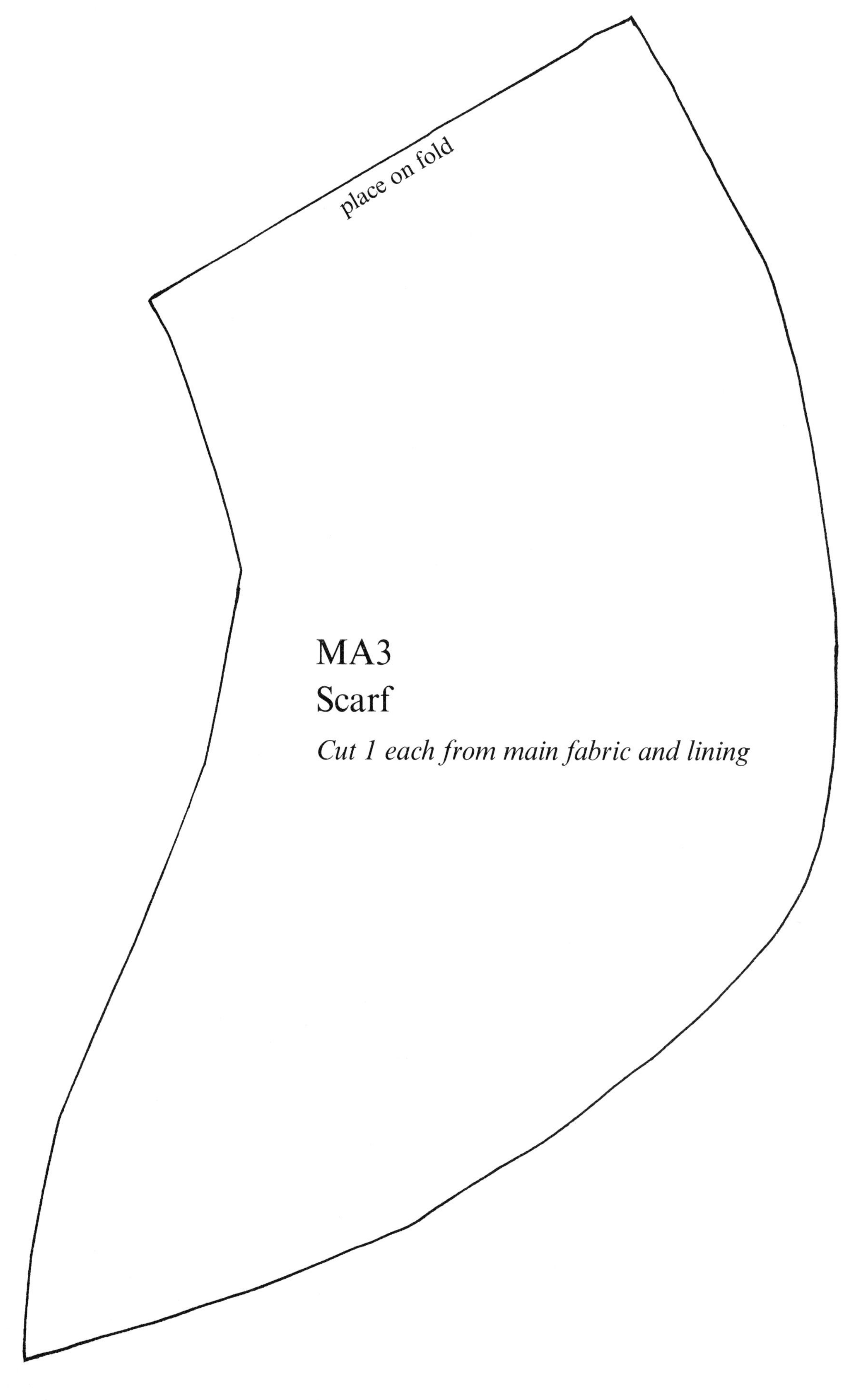
place on fold
MA3
Scarf
Cut 1 each from main fabric and lining

Plate 10

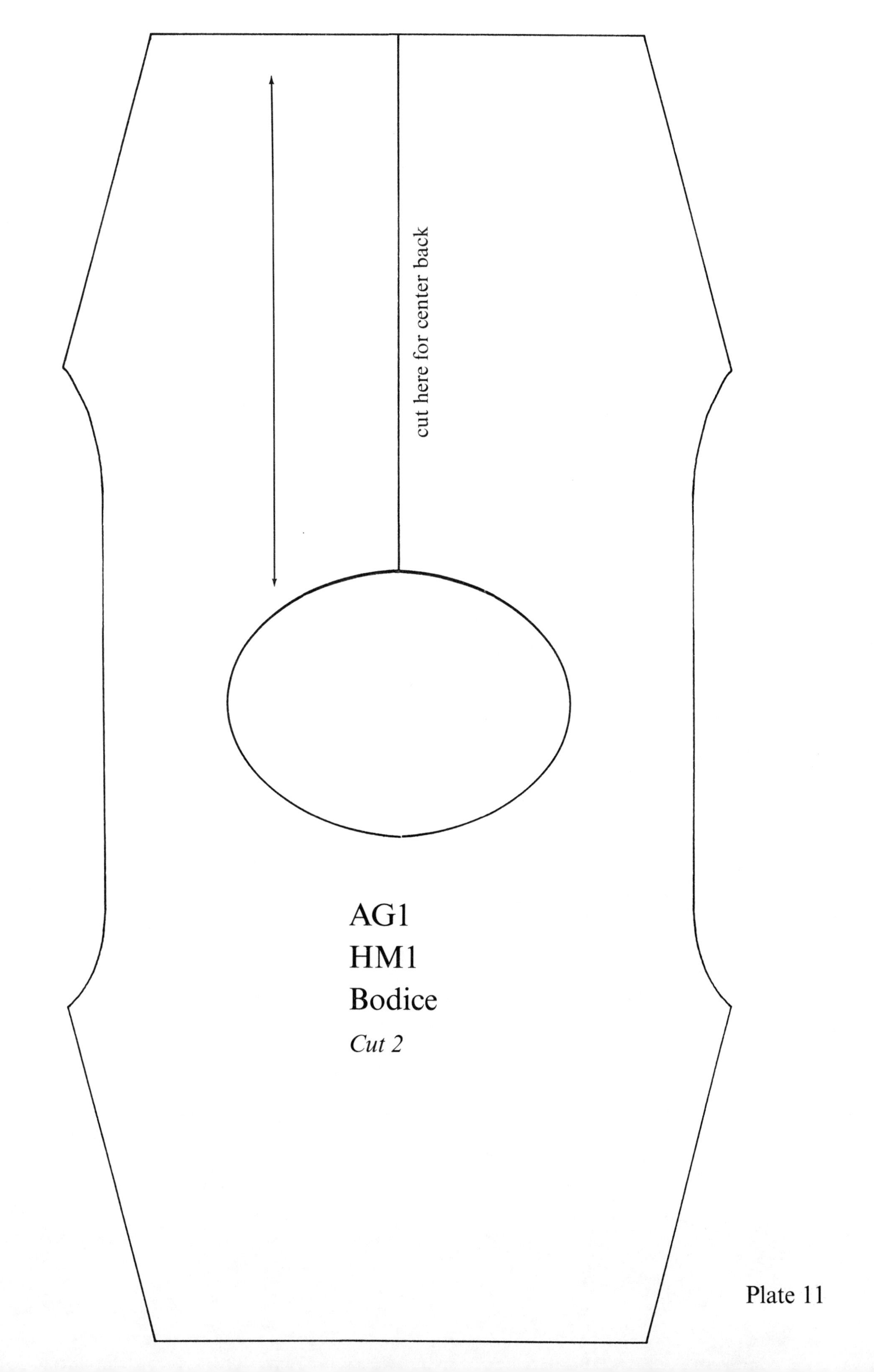
cut here for center back
AG1
HM1
Bodice
Cut 2

front
AG3
Hat
Cut 2 from fabric
Cut 1 from cardboard

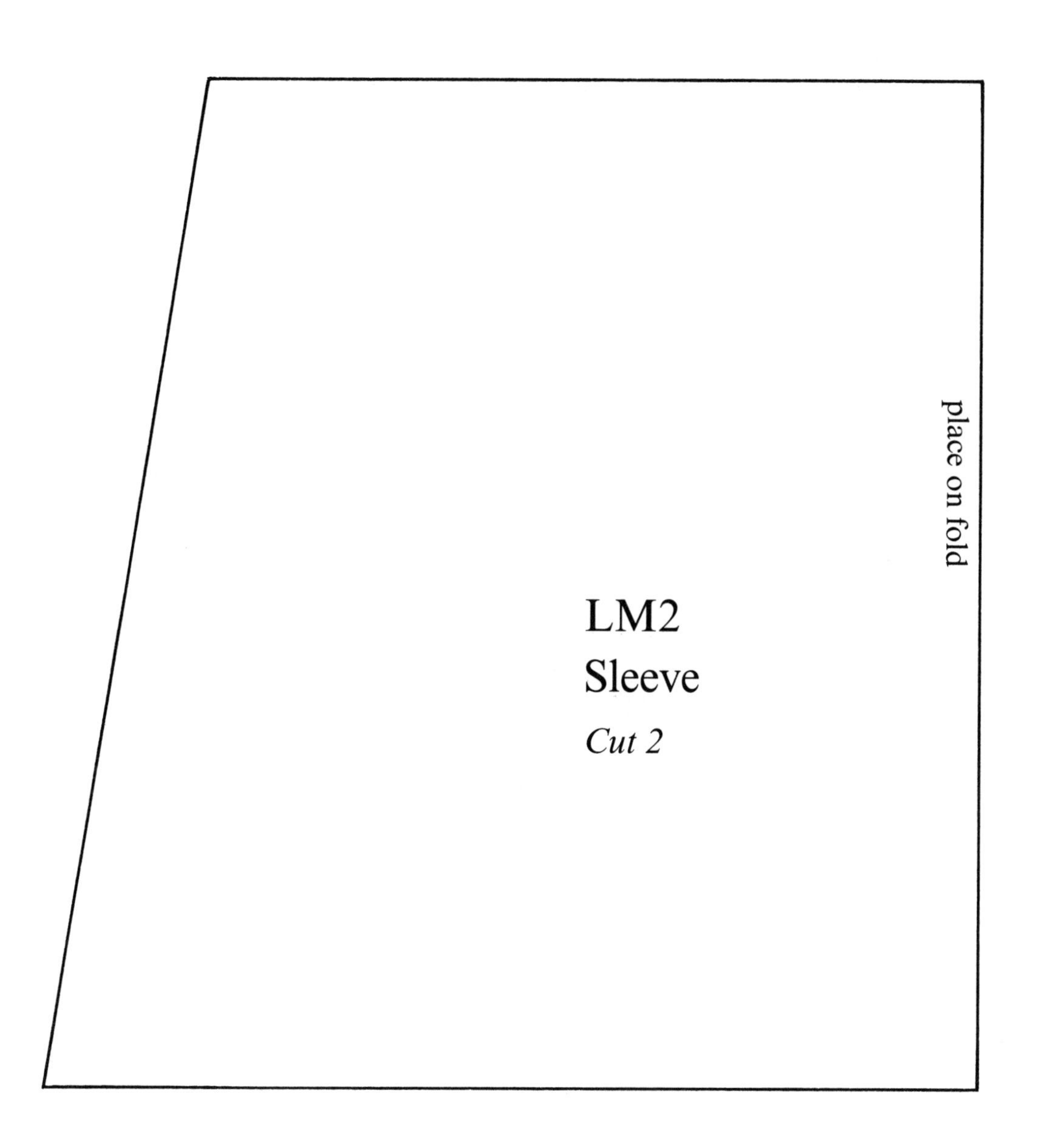


LM3
Cuff
*Cut 2*

fold

Plate 13

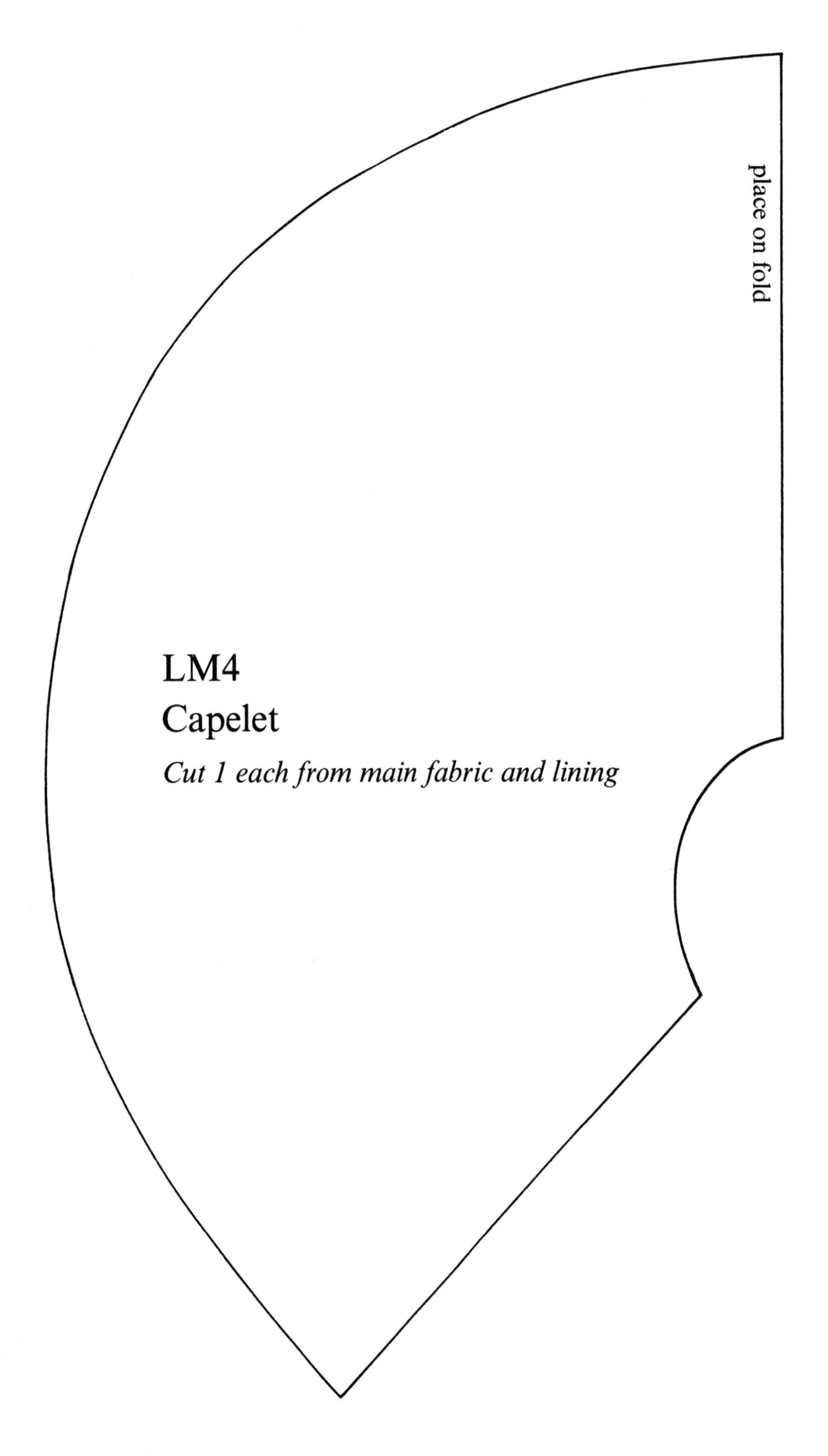
place on fold
LM4
Capelet
Cut 1 each from main fabric and lining

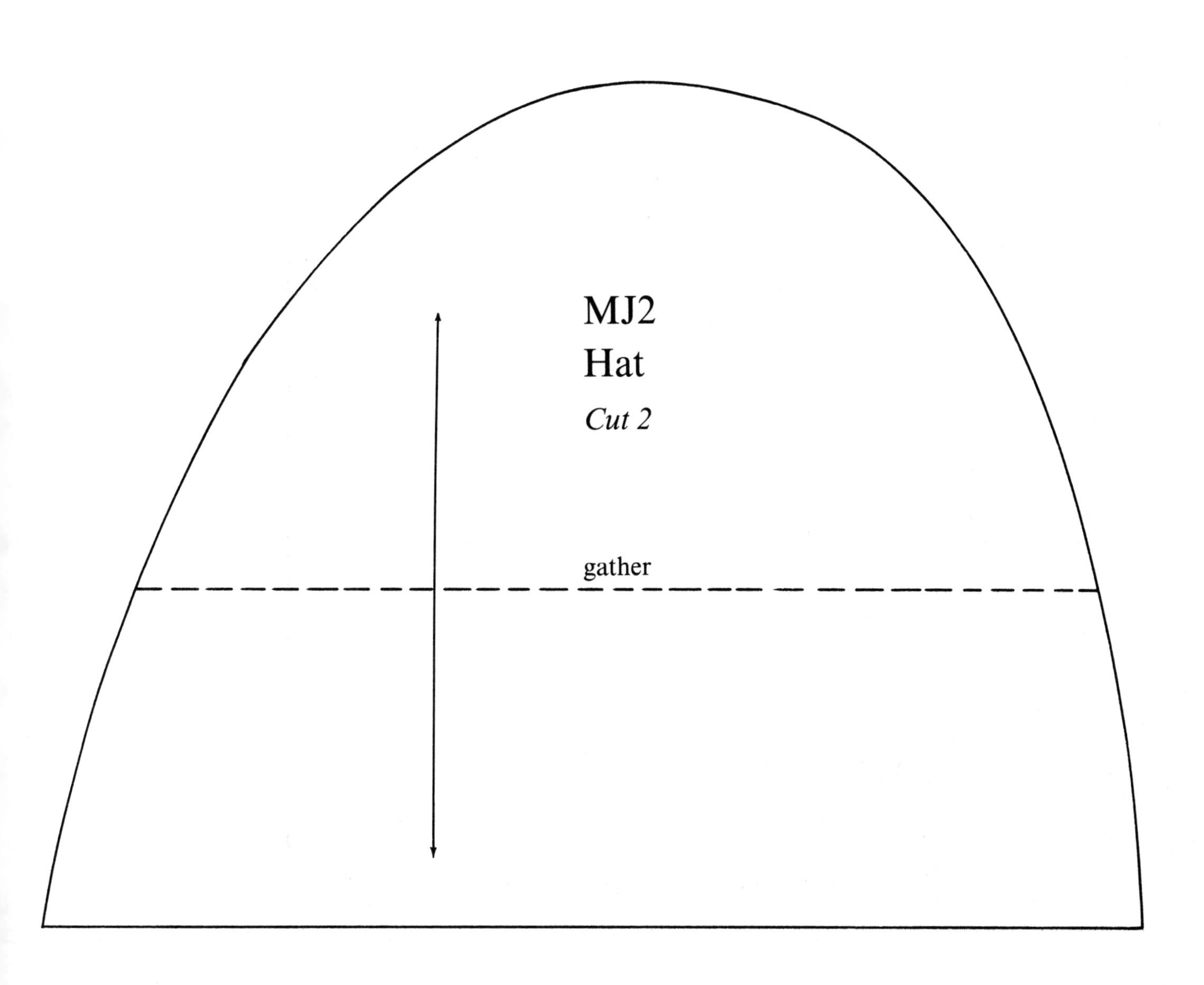
MJ2
Hat
Cut 2
gather

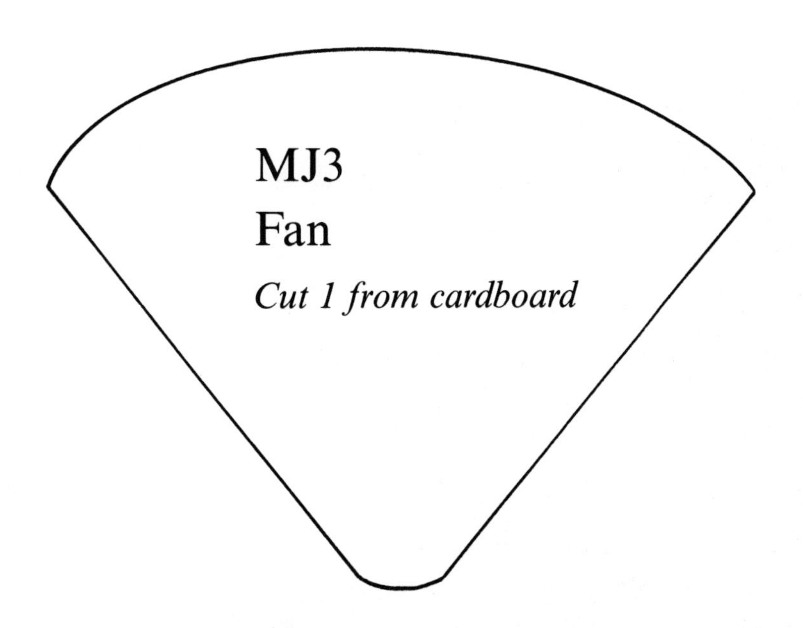
MJ3
Fan
Cut 1 from cardboard

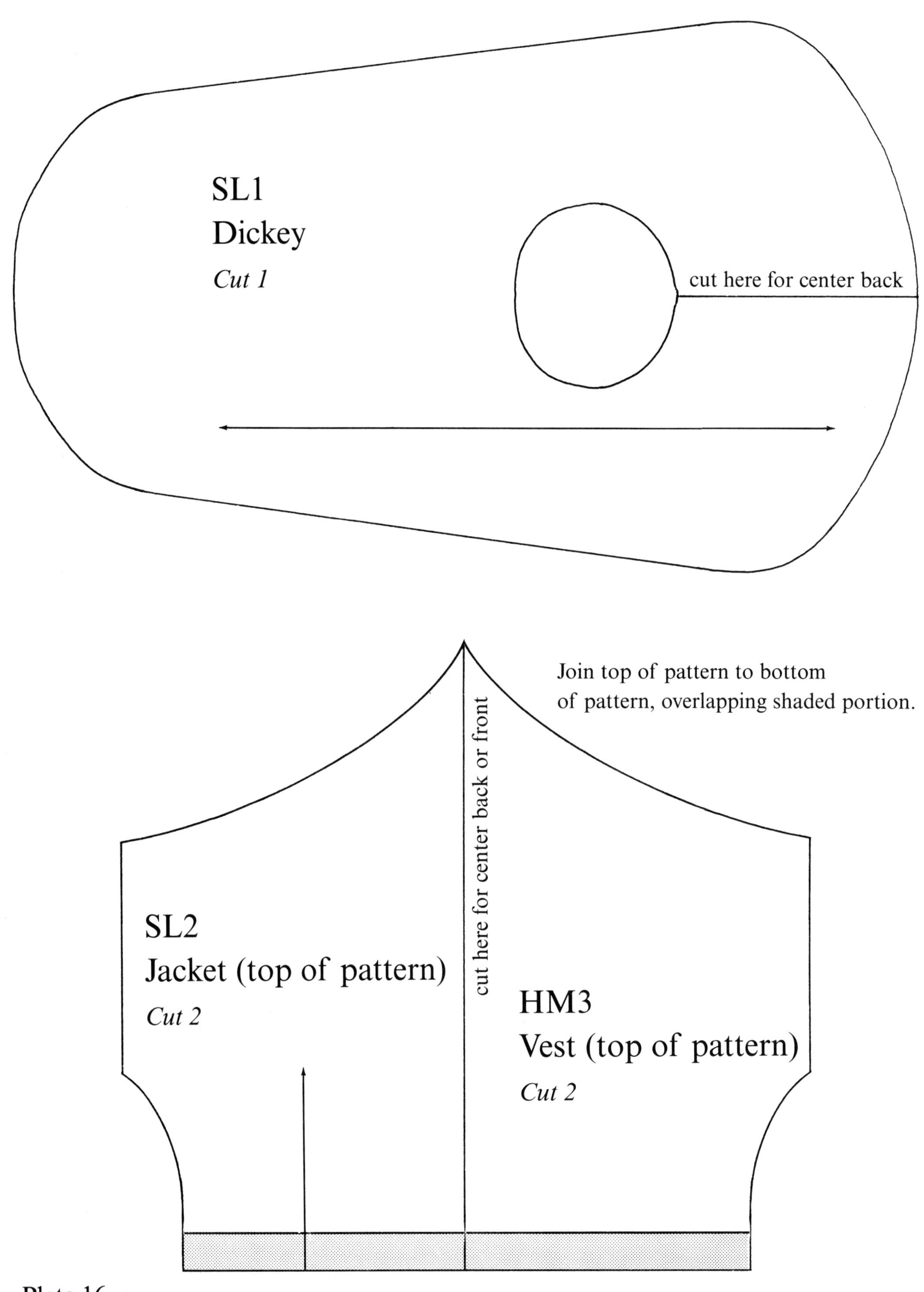
SL1
Dickey
Cut 1
cut here for center back
Join top of pattern to bottom
of pattern, overlapping shaded portion.
cut here for center back or front
SL2
Jacket (top of pattern)
Cut 2
HM3
Vest (top of pattern)
Cut 2

Plate 16

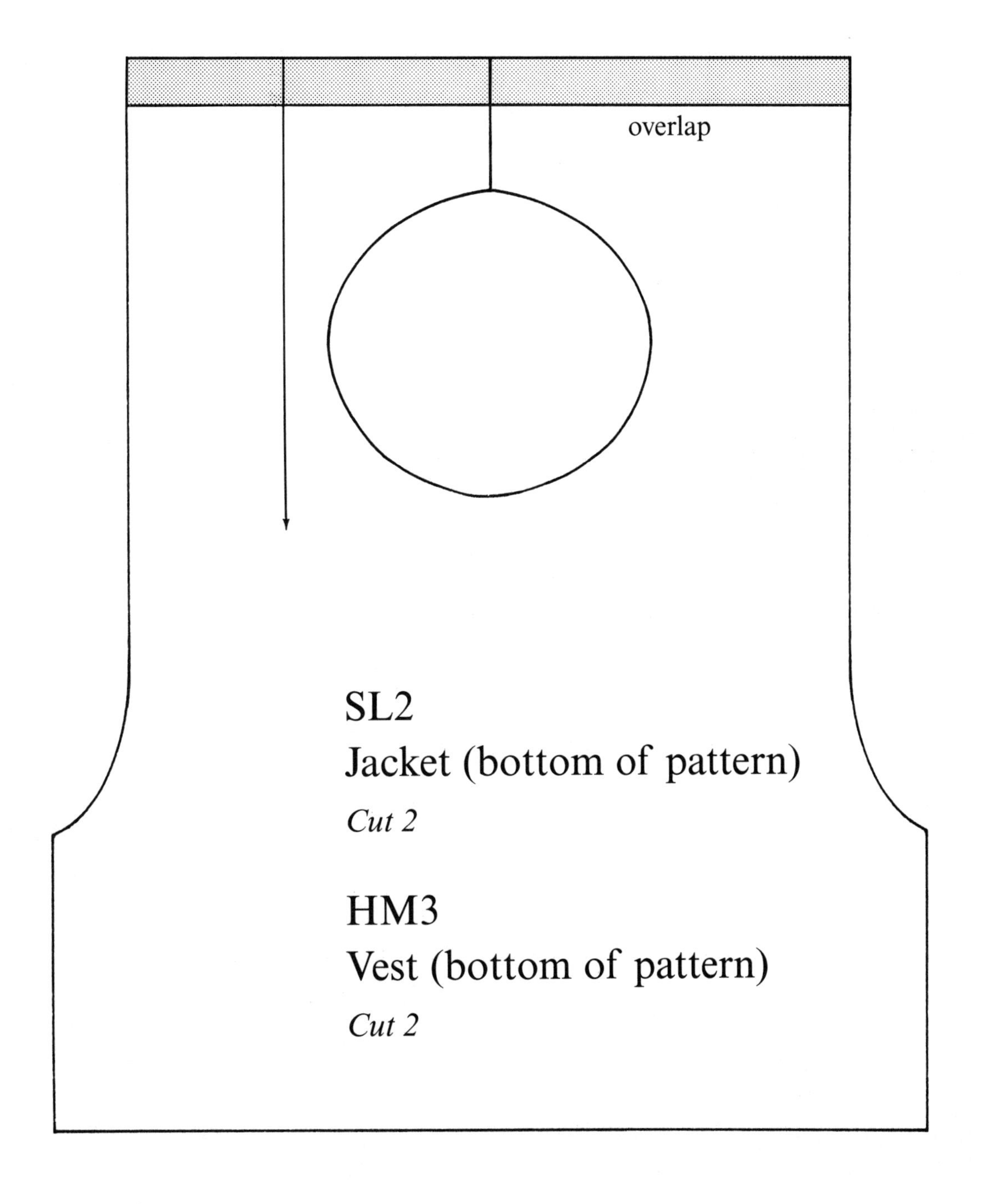
overlap
SL2
Jacket (bottom of pattern)
Cut 2
HM3
Vest (bottom of pattern)
Cut 2

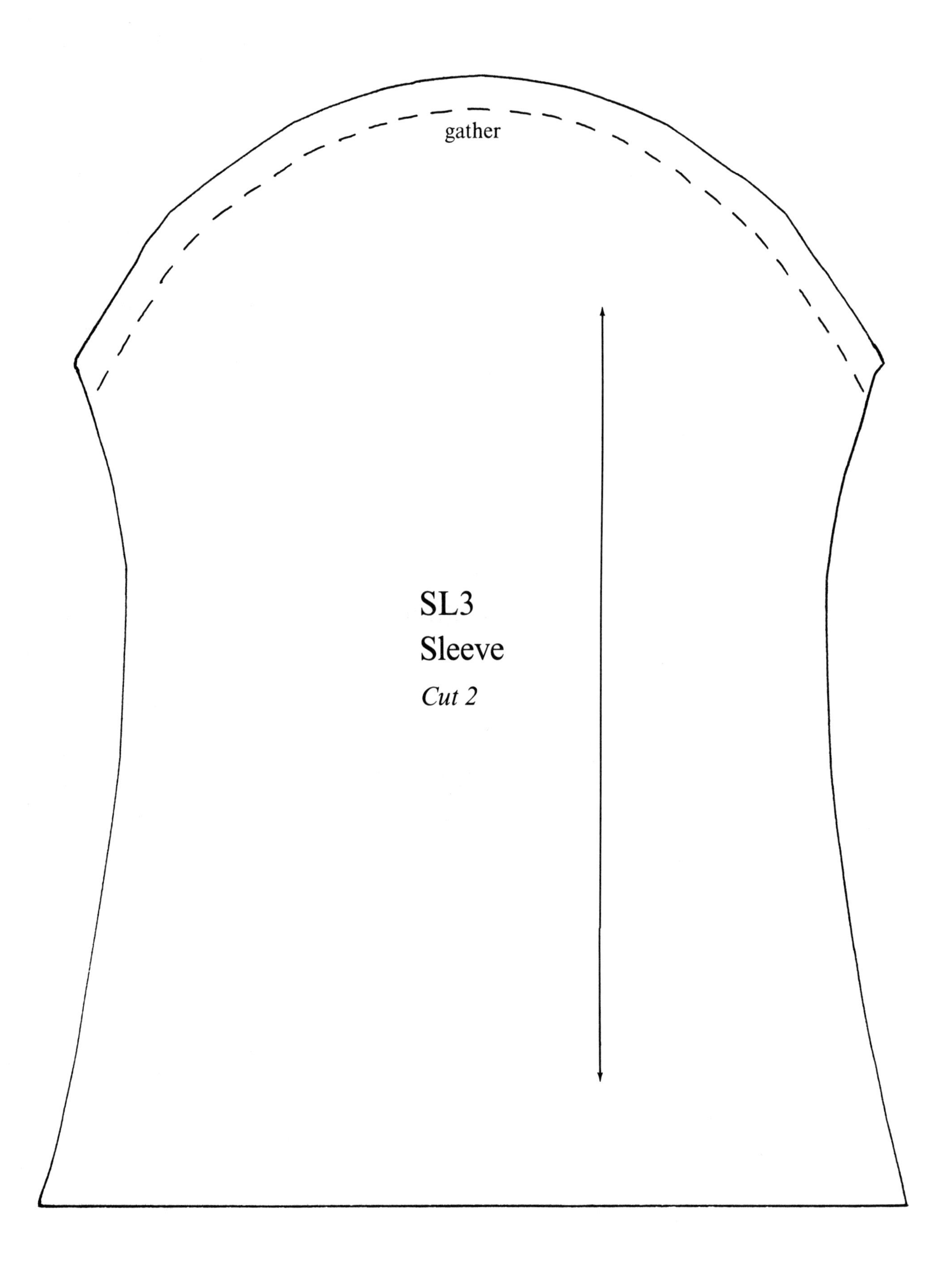
gather
SL3
Sleeve
*Cut 2*

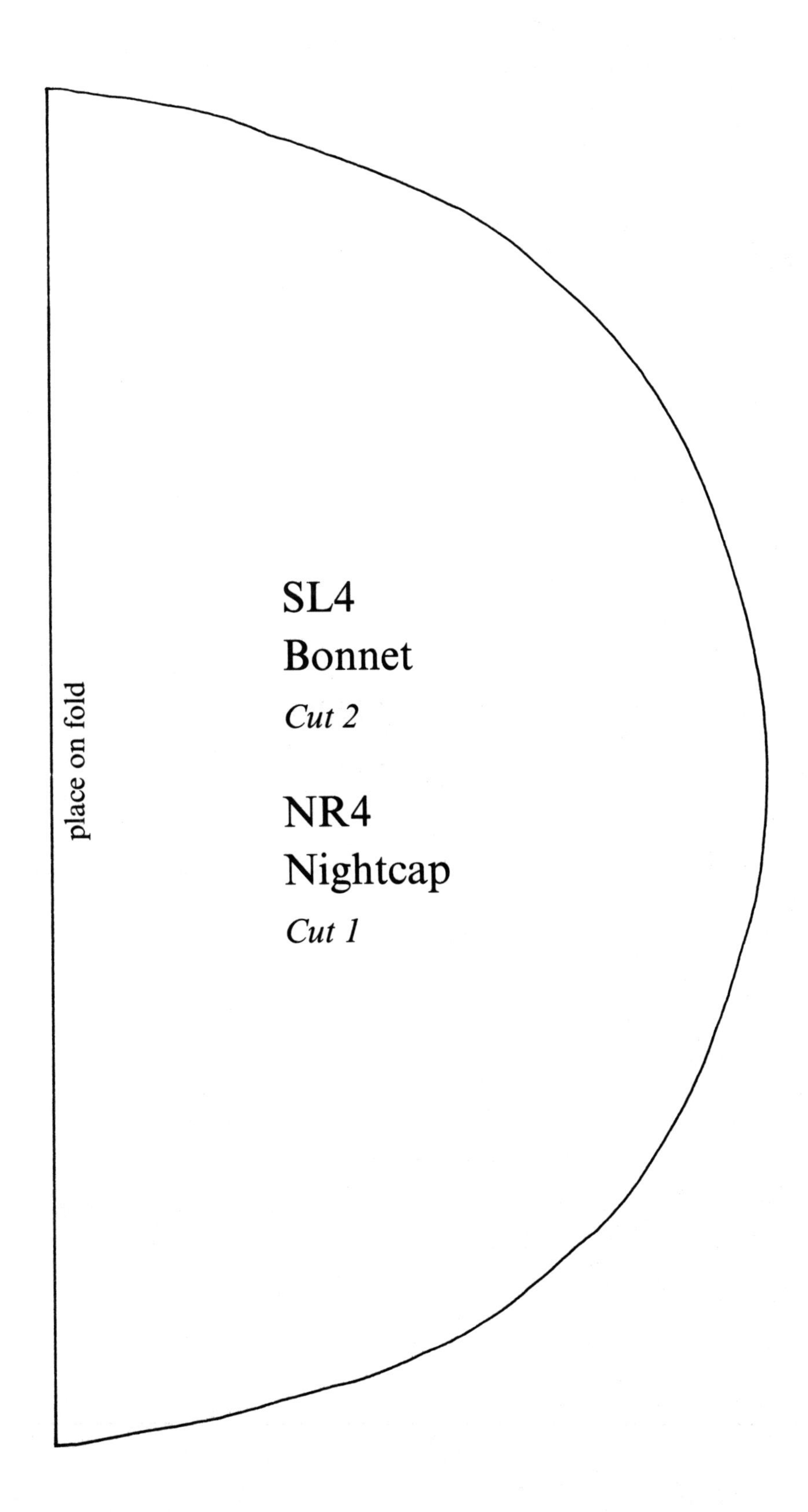
place on fold
SL4
Bonnet
Cut 2
NR4
Nightcap
Cut 1

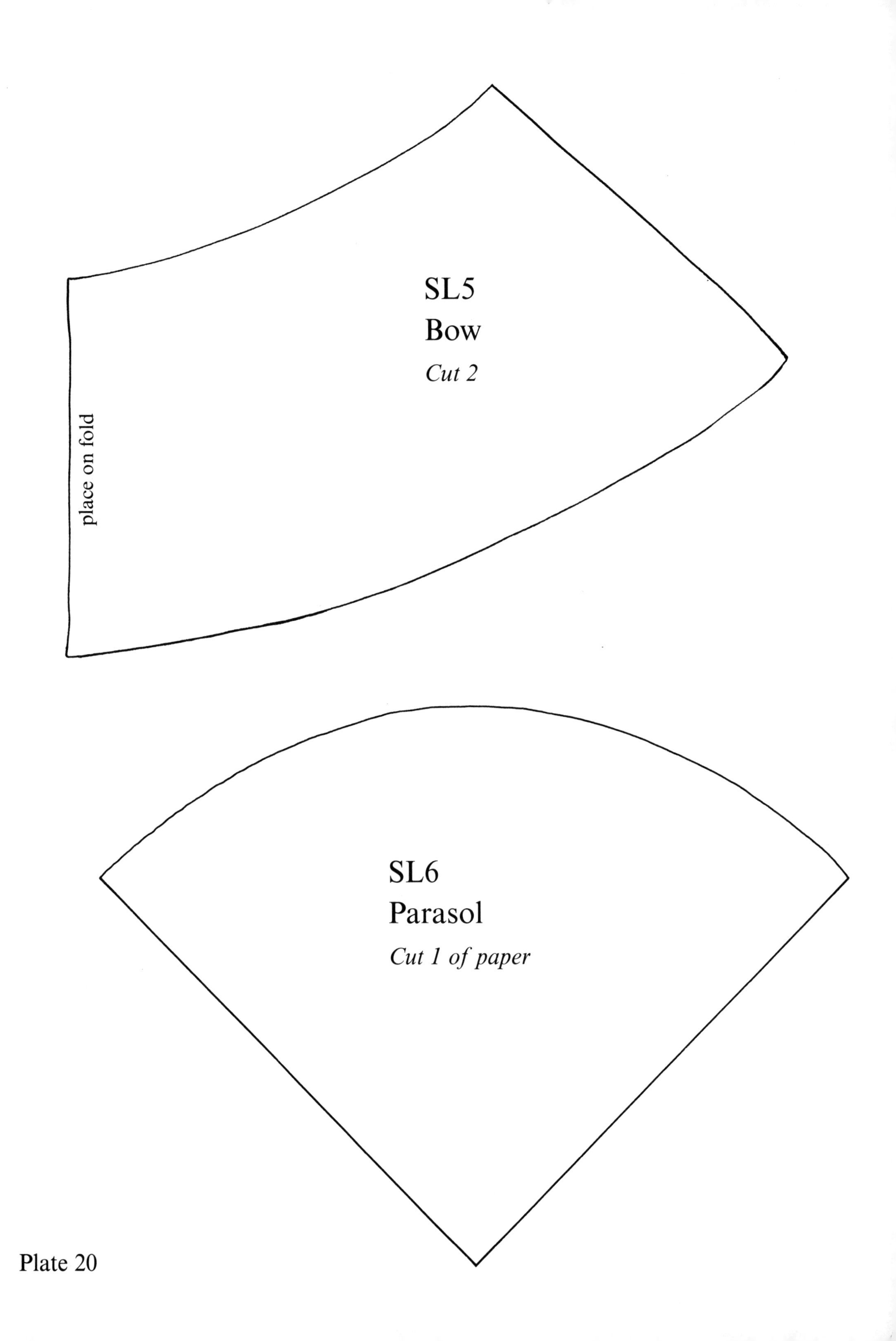
SL5
Bow
Cut 2
place on fold
SL6
Parasol
Cut 1 of paper

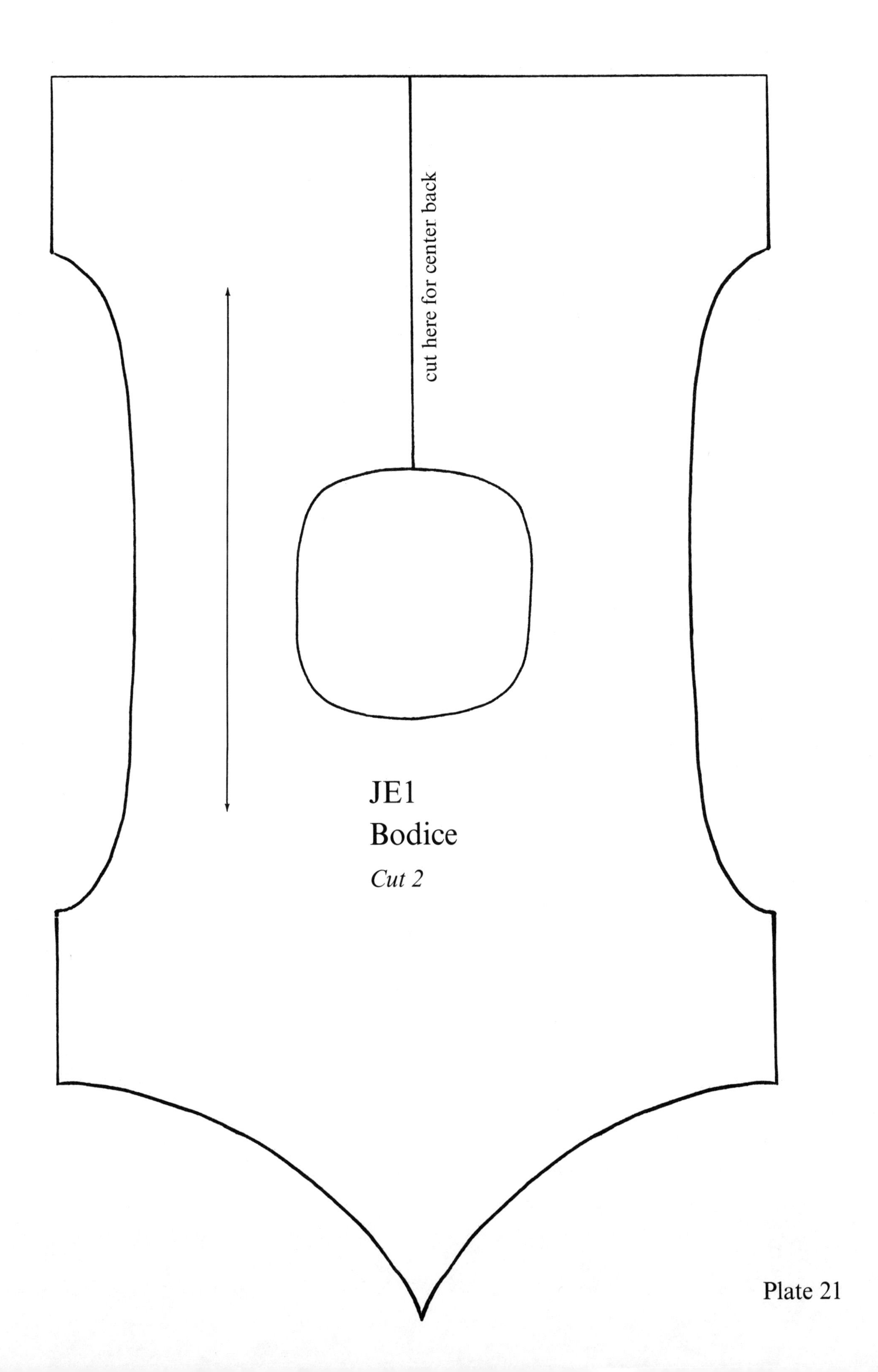
cut here for center back
JE1
Bodice
Cut 2

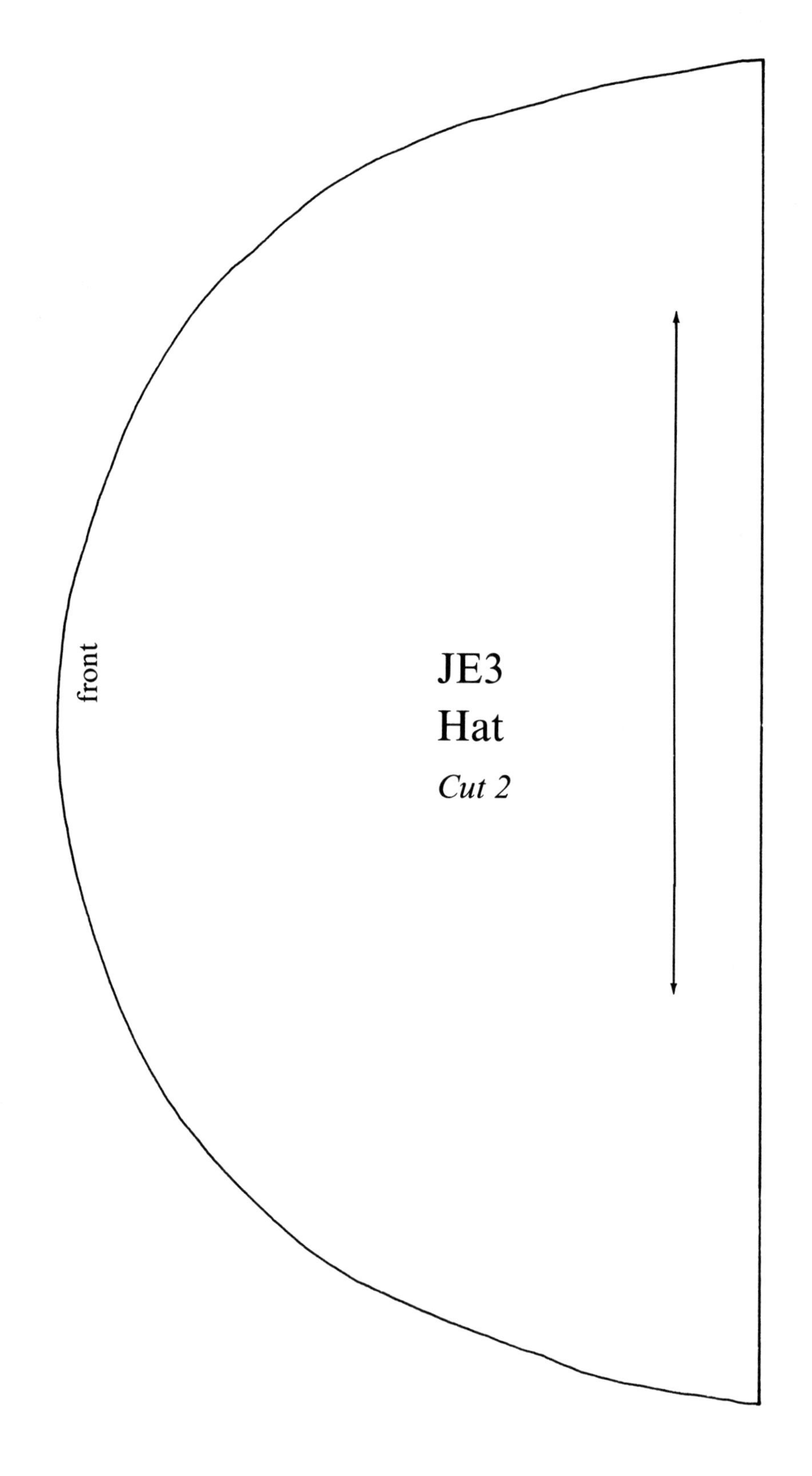
front
JE3
Hat
Cut 2

gather
JE2
NR2
Sleeve
*Cut 2*

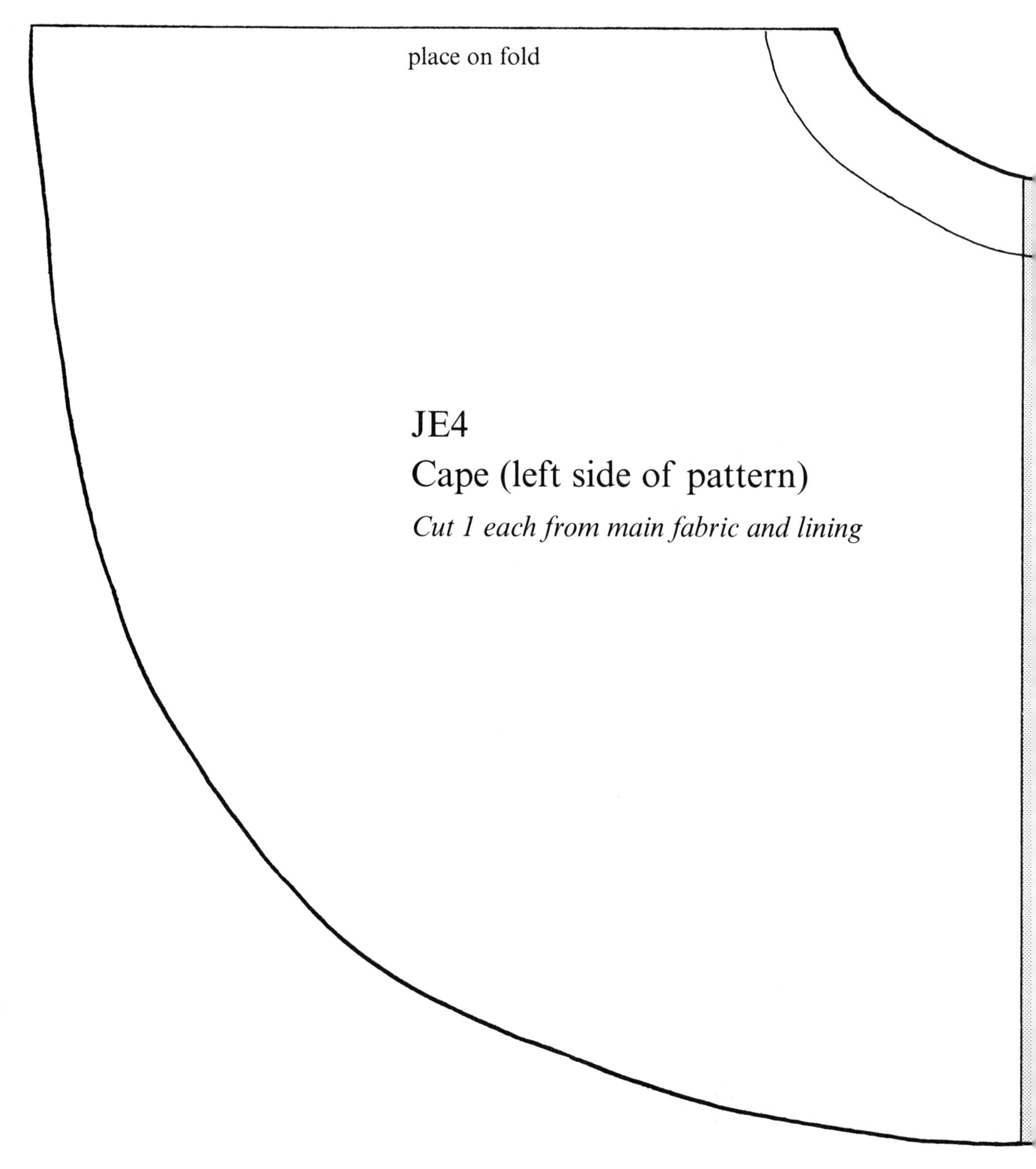


Join left side of pattern to right side of pattern, overlapping shaded portion.

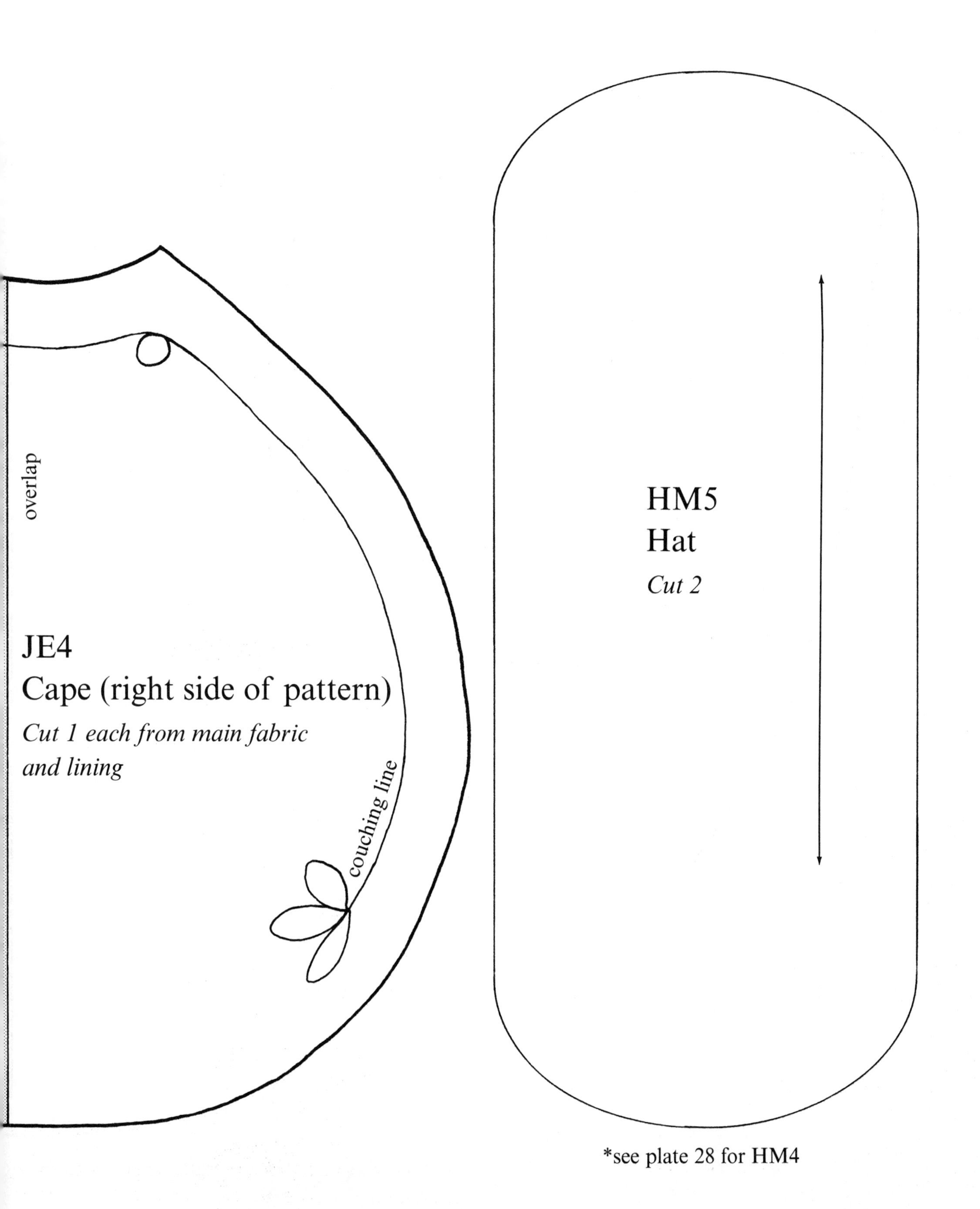


*see plate 28 for HM4

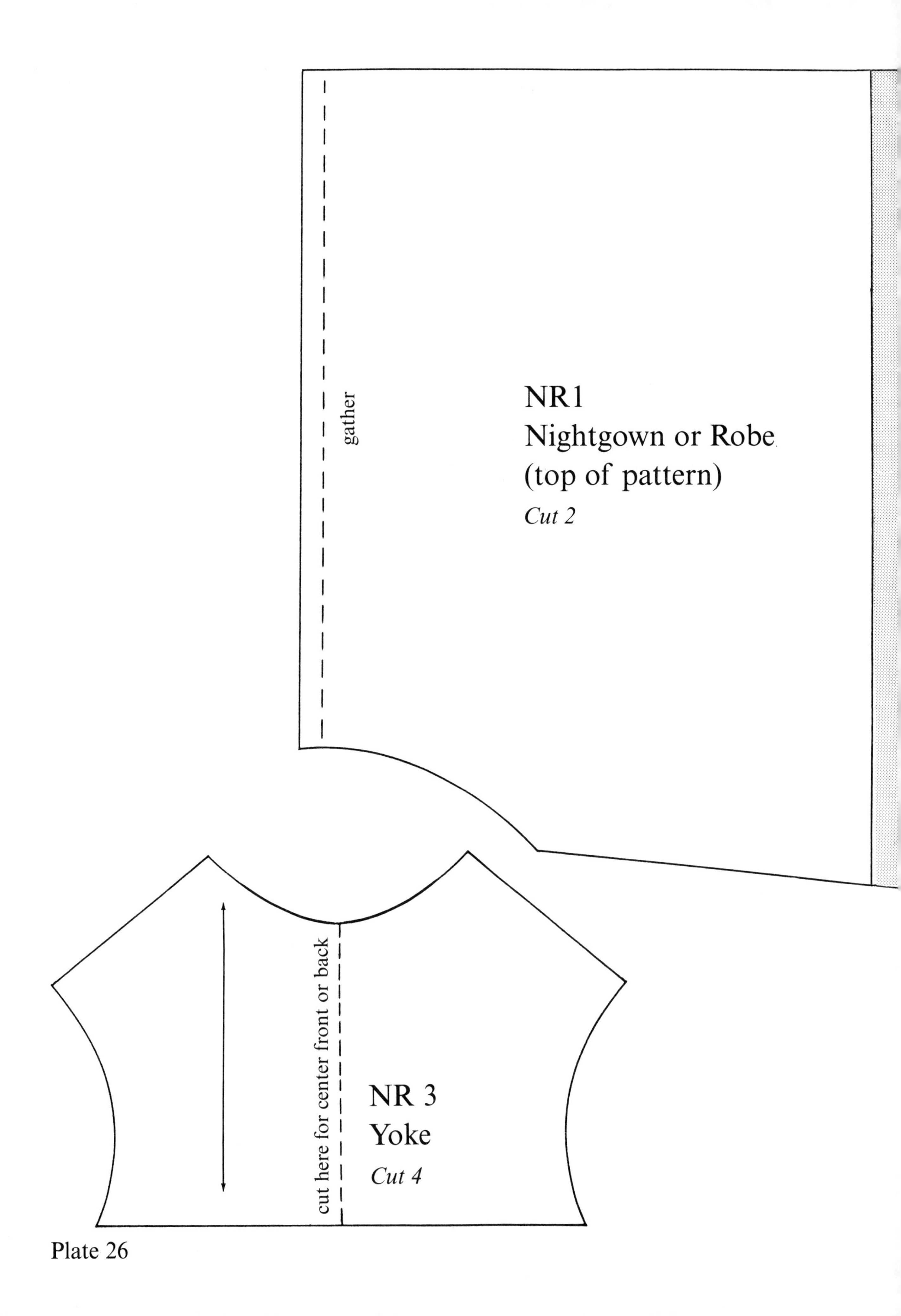
gather
NR1
Nightgown or Robe
(top of pattern)
Cut 2
cut here for center front or back
NR 3
Yoke
Cut 4

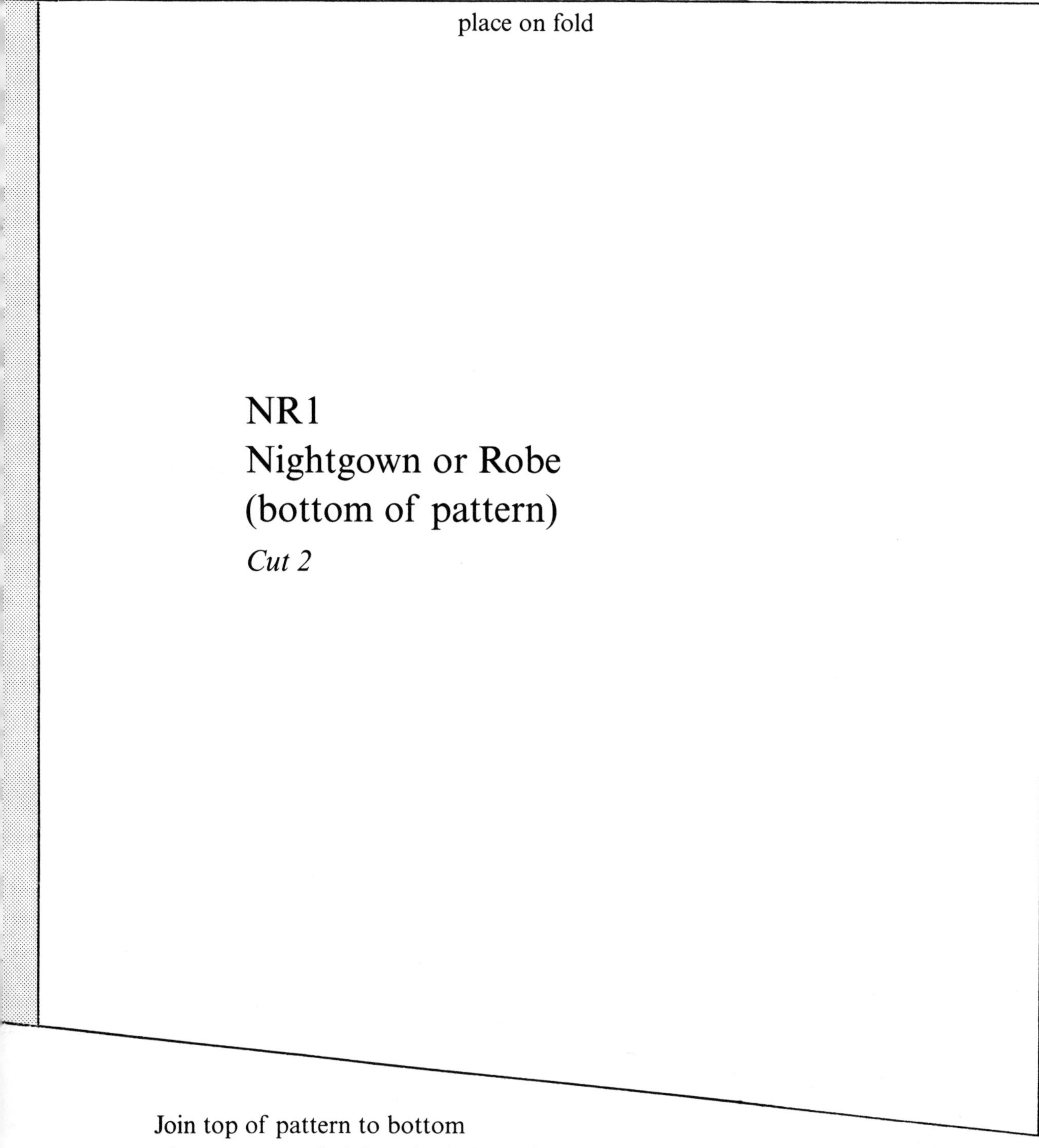


Join top of pattern to bottom
of pattern, overlapping shaded portion.

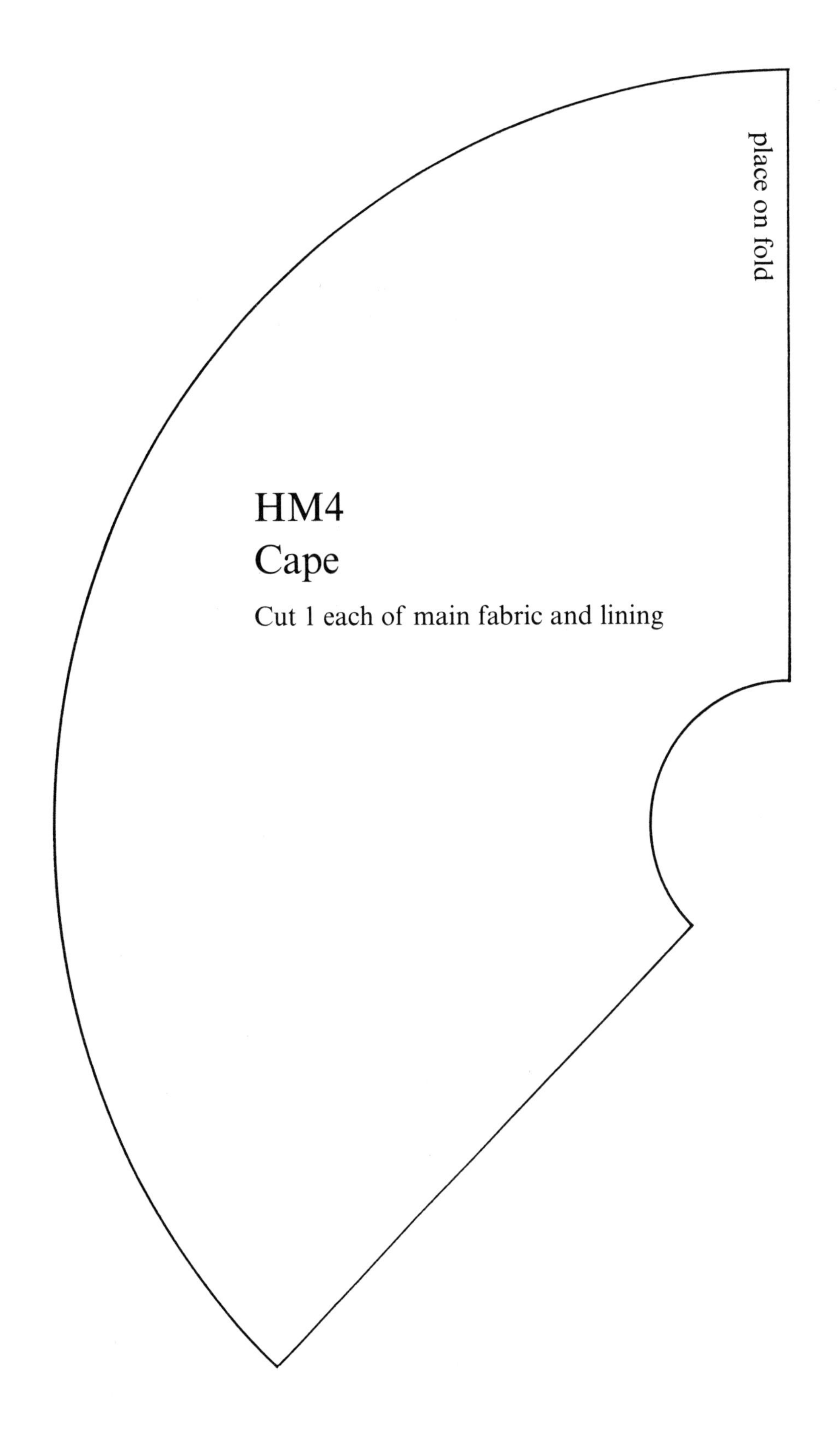
place on fold
HM4
Cape
Cut 1 each of main fabric and lining